Arthur Stanley Cobb

Banks' Cash Reserves

Threadneedle Street

Arthur Stanley Cobb

Banks' Cash Reserves
Threadneedle Street

ISBN/EAN: 9783337096861

Printed in Europe, USA, Canada, Australia, Japan

Cover: Foto ©Suzi / pixelio.de

More available books at **www.hansebooks.com**

BANKS' CASH RESERVES.

THREADNEEDLE STREET

A REPLY TO

"LOMBARD STREET"

(By the late Mr. Walter Bagehot),

And an alternative proposal to the One-pound note scheme sketched by

MR. GOSCHEN AT LEEDS.

BY

ARTHUR STANLEY COBB.

LONDON :

EFFINGHAM WILSON & CO.,

11, ROYAL EXCHANGE.

1891.

CONTENTS.

INTRODUCTION.

THERE are times when a merchant will make almost any sacrifice to obtain ready money. He has entered into no rash speculations, and has only to meet the ordinary legitimate demands of his business, but in order to do so he is suddenly called upon to make a heavy and unexpected loss. To this he gladly submits, for he has been in terror lest no sacrifice could save him from bankruptcy and ruin. But how has this been brought about? Why has he doubted whether his banker would afford him the usual accommodation which when entering into his business engagements he had been relying upon?

Or, take the case of a merchant who has a credit of £50,000 at his bankers. Why is he anxious?

The answer in both cases is that there is a run upon the banks and there is a scarcity of cash.

Such a time, Mr. Goschen speaking at Leeds on the 28th January, and referring to the "Baring crisis," told us we had " only escaped by the skin of our teeth." He said "No fertile imagination could exaggerate the gravity of the crisis, and if I attempt to bring home to those who are listening to me now the serious nature of the crisis, I do so in order to accentuate the necessity of their turning their attention to what I may call the necessity for soundness in our banking and soundness in our currency transactions. I doubt whether the public has thoroughly realised the extent of the danger to which what is called the banking crisis exposed us all. It was not a question of a narrow circle of financiers or traders. The liabilities were so gigantic, the position of the house was so unique, that interests were at stake far beyond individual fortunes, far beyond the fortunes of any class. We were on the brink of a crisis through which it might have been difficult for the soundest to pass unscathed, for the

wealthiest to have escaped. It was a time
when none who had liabilities or engagements
to pay could say how they could pay them if
a condition of things were to continue under
which securities could not be realised, under
which produce could not be sold, under which
bills could not be discounted, under which there
appeared an absence of cash sufficient to discharge the liabilities of the general public."

This suggests the question—Is there no cash
reserve kept for such an emergency?

It is impossible to conceive anything more unsatisfactory than the reply—The Bank of England
keeps the only " Cash reserve," but whether it is
only applicable to the claims of its depositors, or
whether it is also kept for the purpose of making
advances upon securities to anyone who may
apply for them in an emergency, is an open
question. It has been contended on behalf of
the Bank of England that it is not kept for this
latter purpose, but on the part of the other
banks it is maintained that it is. Yet this is the
exact position in which the controversy as to
banks' " cash reserves " is left.

After the last panic, brought about by the failure of Overend and Gurney, the " Economist" in criticising the speech of the Governor of the Bank of England at the next meeting of its proprietors, said that " it acknowledged the ' duty' on the part of the Bank of England to support the ' banking community,' to make the reserve of the Bank do for them as well as itself," and that "the Bank agrees in fact, if not in name, to make unlimited advances, on proper security, to anyone who applies for it." Mr. Bagehot in his " Lombard Street," p. 168, says :—" This article was much disliked by many of the Bank directors, and especially by some whose opinion is of great authority. They thought that the ' Economist' drew ' rash deductions ' from a speech which was in itself ' open to some objection,'—which was like all such speeches, defective in theoretical precision, and which was at best only the expression of an opinion by the Governor of that day, which had not been authorised by the Court of Directors, which could not bind the Bank. However, the article had at least this use, that it brought out the facts. All the directors would have felt a difficulty in commenting upon, or limiting, or in differing from, a speech of a Governor from the chair. But there was no difficulty or delicacy in attacking the 'Economist.' Accordingly, Mr. Hankey, one of the most experienced bank directors, not long after, took occasion to observe :—

" The 'Economist' newspaper has put forth what, in my opinion, is the most mischievous doctrine ever broached in the monetary or banking world in this country; viz., that it is the proper function of the Bank of England to keep money available at all times to supply the demands of bankers who had rendered their own assets unavailable. Until such a doctrine is repudiated by the banking interest, the difficulty of pursuing any sound principle of banking in London will be always very great. But I do not believe that such a doctrine as that bankers are justified in relying on the Bank of England to assist them in time of need, is generally held by the bankers in London."

If Mr. Hankey's statement had been accepted there would have been an end of the controversy,

and after the next panic it could not be asked, as
it was in the "Economist" of 22nd Sept., 1866 :
" Let us know precisely who is to keep the Bank
reserve. If the Joint Stock Banks and the Private
Banks and the Country Banks are to keep their
share, let us determine on that; Mr. Gladstone
appeared not long since to say in Parliament
that it ought to be so. But at any-rate there
should be no doubt whose duty it is."· But
Mr. Hankey's statement was not received as final,
and Mr. Bagehot published " Lombard Street "
to show why it was not.

As Mr. Bagehot's work is called "Lombard
Street," I venture to call this book—in which it
is asserted that he has not proved that it is the
duty of the "Old Lady of Threadneedle Street"
to save Lombard Street bankers the trouble and
expense of keeping cash reserves—"Threadneedle
Street "

THREADNEEDLE STREET.

CHAPTER I.

THE proposition that it is the duty of the Bank
of England to keep money available at all times
to supply the demands of bankers who have
rendered their own assets unavailable, when
stated in this explicit manner, appears on the
face of it so utterly unreasonable, that it suggests an enquiry into the circumstances which
could have produced it. If anyone nowadays
were to sit down and elaborate a plan on which
banking should be conducted, it would not occur
to him to establish in London only one bank,
and confer upon it the privilege of exclusive
banking. Such a proposal would be so entirely
out of harmony with the notions of to-day that
it is necessary to be reminded that the object of
founding the Bank of England was to raise
money for the use of the Government. The

Act of Parliament by which the Bank was
established in 1694 is entitled "An Act for
granting to their Majesties several duties upon
tonnage of ships and vessels, and upon beer, ale,
and other liquors, for securing certain recom-
penses and advantages in the said Act men-
tioned, to such persons as shall voluntarily
advance the sum of fifteen hundred thousand
pounds towards carrying on the war with
France." From time to time the charter of
the Bank of England was renewed, and with
it the privilege of exclusive banking was granted.
During the existence of this privilege no Banking
Company of more than six persons was allowed
to issue notes payable on demand within London
or 65 miles thereof. The notes so issued were
payable in cash on demand, until 1797, when the
suspension of cash payments took place under an
order in council, based upon a report from the
Chancellor of the Exchequer that an unusual
demand for specie had been made upon the
Metropolis, in consequence of ill-founded or ex-
aggerated alarms in different parts of the country;
and it appeared that unless some measure was
immediately taken there might have been reason
to apprehend a want of a sufficient supply of cash

to answer the exigencies of the public service. This order in council was followed by the Bank Restriction Act (in the first instance passed for a period of 52 days, but which continued in force for 22 years), which provided that the Bank of England should not be sued for the payment of any of their notes for which they were willing to give other notes ; and that no person could be held to special bail upon any process issuing out of any court, unless the affidavit made for the purpose stated, also, that the party had made no offer to pay in bank notes. The result was that bank notes were constantly at a discount, and the Bullion Committee in 1810 reported to the House of Commons " there is at present an excess in the paper circulation of this country which is to be ascribed to the want of a sufficient check and control in the issues of paper from the Bank of England, and originally to the suspension of cash payments which removed the natural and true control." However, the House rejected their report, and, in their collective wisdom, came to the conclusion that it was not the value of bank notes that was depreciated, but that the value of gold was advanced—in other words that the promise of a bank note to pay so many pounds on demand

was of not less value than the actual payment of
the metal, although only a smaller amount of
the metal than was promised by the note could
be obtained for it! Nine years afterwards cash
payments were resumed. In January 7th, 1824,
the Bank held £14,200,000 of bullion. By
November, 1825, the amount was reduced to
£1,300,000. Up to this time the Directors did
not apparently realise the possibility of danger,
when they suddenly became alarmed, and on
their diminishing the circulation forthwith to the
extent of £3,500,000, a panic occurred. They
applied to the Government to again restrain payments in gold, but the Government refused to do
so. They then adopted another policy, and
instead of diminishing the circulation they lent
by every possible means, and in modes never
before adopted. The bullion was reduced to
£1,260,890—the notes were all issued—and the
Bank was on the eve of suspending payment,
when a box containing a quantity of one pound
notes, which had been accidentally overlooked
when all notes under £5 had been called in, was
discovered. That box of paper is said to have
saved the credit of the country. In 1836 and
1839 the Bank's position was again jeopardised,

and in the latter year the directors had to resort
to the Paris bankers for a loan of two millions.
By this time the country was thoroughly dis-
satisfied with the conduct of banks, and legislation was imperatively demanded. After a long
controversy, the Bank Charter Act of 1844 which
lays down the conditions upon which bank notes
are now issued was passed; the Bank of England
was divided into two distinct departments—the
Issue and the Banking; and the relations of the
Government to the Bank (except as customers of
the Bank in the ordinary way) were confined to
their responsibility to the Issue Department for
the loan due from the country to the Bank, upon
the security of which a portion of the notes are
issued.

The " City," however, did not appreciate the
import of the change effected by the Bank Charter
Act 1844 in the relations of the Government and
the Bank of England. Men who had been accus-
tomed to look upon the Bank of England as
specially privileged; who had seen it empowered
to make an unlimited number of promises to pay
on demand which it was absolved from the
necessity of carrying out; could not realise that
it was entirely shorn of its privileges, and that

it no longer had the power to manufacture 'legal tender' with which to assist them in times of difficulty and pressure. The "City" still considered that the Bank of England owed a duty to the public of an altogether different character to that of any other Bank, and the directors of the Bank of England were not backward in acknowledging it. The case of the other banks was placed before the Select Committee on "Commercial Distress" 1847-8 by Mr. R. C. L. Bevan, who was examined as follows:—(Rept. Select Com. Commercial Distress, 1847-8—vol. viii.):—

Query 2384: Do you consider that the Bank directors, appointed by the proprietors to manage their affairs, ought to regulate their affairs to the greatest advantage of their proprietors? No; in that position of public trust which they occupy as holding the public monies, and what are called "private deposits," which are virtually the monies of the public, I do not think they are at liberty to consider only the interests of their proprietors.

Query 2385: Are you aware that when the Act of 1844 passed it was stated in Parliament that the object was twofold; first to create a bank of issue, and secondly to create a bank of deposit; and that the bank directors should be at perfect liberty to act for their own interest as the directors of any other bank would be? I have often heard that stated; I remember hearing it stated at the time, but I thought it was a very great mistake.

Query 2386: You think that was not a good plan? I think it was most unsound in principle; certainly it was acted upon by the Bank; I think they took those parties at their word.

Query 2389: Do not you consider that the bank directors ought to attend to the interest of their proprietors in the same manner as you would to your own interest? No; because they are a public bank in a way and in a sense in which we are not.

Query 2390: Where is the distinction now that a separation has taken place between the two departments, and that the discount branch is separated entirely from the issue branch? They hold a great many Government deposits.

Query 2391: But they only hold the deposits of the Government in the same way as you hold the deposits of various public companies; they may be greater in amount, but in principle are not they the same? I think that the Bank are bankers to the public in a sense in which we are not; not only to a much larger amount, but that they occupy a position evidently that we do not occupy, involving a trust which does not devolve upon us.

Query 2392: You consider that to be a trust different from what you as bankers have? I think we have a right to do as we please, but I do not think that the Bank has; if we please to withhold all accommodation we should have a right to do so, but I do not think the Bank have that right.

The Governor of the Bank of England (Mr. James Morris), and the Deputy Governor (Mr. Henry James Prescott), were asked the following questions:—

Query 2653: With regard to the banking department in what condition did the Act place you? It placed the Bank of England in the condition of any other bank, except that we were carrying on business upon a much larger scale, and we had also Government deposits to deal with.

Query 2654: It has been stated that the effect of the Act of 1844, was to relieve you

from any other responsibility than that which
you had to your own proprietors, with the view
of making the dividend for them as large as
it could be made; do you consider that the Bank
was relieved from all responsibility, as regards
the banking department, with reference to the
public interest? I may state that as far as the
Bank was concerned, I think the Bank ought
to have been carried on exactly on the same
principle as that established by the Act of 1844;
whether the Act of 1844 had passed or not, we
ought to have had a separation of the two departments; the issue department will naturally take
care of itself; with respect to the banking
department we have a duty to the public to
perform, and a duty to perform to the proprietors; our duty to our proprietors would lead us
to make the best dividend we could for them;
but in doing that we are bound to take care,
considering the power that the Bank have as a
large body, not to interfere generally with the
monetary affairs of the country. I have always
considered that the two interests were united,
the proprietors' interest and the public interest;
I have always found that whenever a step has
been taken to promote the interests of the pro-

prietors at the cost of the public it has invariably fallen back upon us, and instead of bettering ourselves we have put ourselves in a worse position. (Mr. Prescott): I should say that in all the more important measures of the Bank, such as in reducing or raising the rate of interest, the first thing the directors look to is the public interest rather than the interest of the proprietors of the Bank.

The Committee reported upon the matter as follows :—First Rept. from Sel. Com. 8th June, 1848—p. iv. :—

" An opinion seems to have been entertained by some persons, though not by the Governor and Deputy Governor of the Bank of England, that the Bank is released by the Act of 1844, from any obligation except that of consulting the pecuniary interests of its proprietors. It is true that there are no restrictions imposed by law upon the discretion of the Bank in respect to the conduct of the banking, as distinguished from the issue department. But the Bank is a public institution, possessed of special and exclusive privileges, standing in a peculiar relation to the Government, and exercising from the magnitude of its resources great influence over the general mercantile and monetary transactions of the country. These circumstances impose upon the Bank the duty of a consideration of the public interest, not indeed enacted or defined by law, but which Parliament in its various transactions with the Bank has always recognised, and which the Bank has never disclaimed. It is unnecessary to impose such duty by law as there can be little doubt that the permanent interests of the Bank are identified with those of the public at large."

A more ambiguous report could not have been devised. It asserts that circumstances have imposed upon the Bank " the duty of a consideration of the public interest," but of the nature of that duty it says nothing. The circumstances which are said to impose that duty are (1), the Bank is a "public institution," but no explanation is given of the applicability of that description. It is certainly not carried on for the benefit of the public, but for the benefit of its proprietors in the same way as any other joint stock bank. (2). It is said to be possessed of "special and exclusive privileges," but the Committee omitted to enumerate them, and since the establishment of the Issue Department the privilege of "exclusive banking" so far as the Banking Department of the Bank of England is concerned has disappeared. (3). Because "it stands in a peculiar relation to the Government," which probably refers to the Government deposits; but what other obligation the Bank has incurred in consequence of being their custodian than to produce them when required, is left to the imagination. (4). Because of "the magnitude of its resources exercising a great influence over the general mercantile and monetary transactions of the country." The greater the power the greater the responsibility; but that is a question of degree, not of principle; and the report does not elucidate why it should be regarded otherwise.

Thus, the report of the Committee does not throw any light upon the nature of the duty of a consideration of the public interest imposed upon the Bank of England. Mr. R. C. L. Bevan, the representative of the other banks, however, had made a very definite statement of what he conceived to be the duty of the Bank as "bankers to the public," and because they "occupied a position evidently that we do not occupy." In his opinion, speaking on behalf of the other banks,

"We have a right to do as we please, but I do not think that the Bank has; if we please to withhold all accommodation we should have a right to do so, but I do not think the Bank have that right." The Committee ought to have dealt with that specific claim. It is a very extraordinary one. In these days the joint stock and other banks are also "bankers to the public," several of the public accounts being kept with them; but they would be rather astonished if they were told that, in consequence, they could no longer do as they pleased with their own funds, the fact of some public accounts being kept with them entitling the public generally to accommodation from them. Or, to apply Mr. Bevan's contention to the case of a country town, it amounts to this, that the bank where the Corporation, or other public body, keeps its account is, in consequence, bound to accommodate the public—not merely their own customers because of their private affairs, but any member of the public because their representatives have made them the "bankers to the public." A *reductio ad absurdum.*

The evidence of the Governor and Deputy Governor of the Bank was very unfortunate.

It cannot be construed as an admission that the
Bank undertook to keep a cash reserve out of
which to supply the demands of Bankers and
others who render their own assets unavailable.
But, in drawing the distinction between the duty
of the Bank to the public and its duty to its
proprietors; in admitting that the Bank had
sometimes taken steps to promote the interests
of the proprietors at the cost of the public ; and
in asserting that the directors in all the more
important measures of the Bank, such as in
reducing or raising the rate of interest, first
looked to the public interest rather than to the
interest of the proprietors of the Bank; the
Governors gave room for the introduction of
all sorts of claims upon them to which it would
have been far better if they had not opened
the door.   However, after saying this much,
what does it amount to ? They stated that the
Banking Department of the Bank of England
was " in the condition of any other bank except
that we were carrying on business upon a much
larger scale, and that we had also the Government deposits "; and they limited their sense
of duty to taking care that the power the Bank
have as a large body should not be used to

"interfere generally with the monetary affairs of the country," and in reducing or raising the rate of interest to "look to the public interest rather than to the interest of the proprietors." They do not admit any peculiar duty arising from the fact that the Bank is the bank of the Government. Their duty arising from their position as the premier bank, vastly superior to its competitors, with the power of controlling the rate of interest, would have been just the same if the Government deposits had been the deposits of an individual.

The claims thus made upon the Banking Department of the Bank of England, and by implication upon its reserve, in consequence of its relations with the Government, are of the most shadowy character; and it is only possible to understand how they could have been entertained for one moment by remembering that the public mind of that day had been educated under a system by which the Bank had enjoyed the privilege of "exclusive banking," and that it had not appreciated the changed conditions brought about by the Bank Charter Act, 1844.

Ten years after this report Mr. Gladstone seemed to think that there were exceptional

relations between the Government and the Banking Department of the Bank of England in
connection with the National Debt. On the
11th December, 1857 (Hansard, p. 652-3) he
said :—

"I do not know whether hon. members are
aware that within the last year or two whenever
you have borrowed any sum of money for the
exigencies of the public service you have like-
wise made a new law that the Bank of England
shall continue to be a Corporation until the whole
of the sum is repaid. What is the meaning of
such a provision? It is quite plain that it is an
enactment drawn from times when governments
were in bad and banks were in good credit;
and when it was a great object of governments,
which used to cheat banks and rob the tills of
traders, to get a body of respectable men to
cover the loans they had contracted. Now I
say such a clause as that in Acts of the present
day is antiquated and superannuated. It is
desirable that those who lend money to the
people of England should know that they do so
on the credit of the State, and that the credit
and the honor of Parliament should not be supple-
mented by such an assurance to our creditors."

If this was the correct explanation of the clause in the "Loan Acts," the affairs of the Government and the Banking Department of the Bank of England would be inextricably intermixed. But the real object and effect of this clause is explained in a paper dated the 10th February, 1858, and delivered to the Committee appointed to consider a proposal for a "State Bank" by the Chancellor of the Exchequer on the 16th March, 1858. It states:—"By the Act 54, Geo. III, cap. 76, and subsequent 'Loan Acts,' the management of the public debt is entrusted to the Bank of England; and the Governor and Company of the Bank of England, and their successors, are continued a Corporation for that purpose until the debt shall be redeemed by Parliament. It would appear to be open to Parliament to put an end to this guarantee by such a reconstitution of the National Debt as would amount to a redemption of the existing Public Annuities. While, however, the debt subsists in its present form, the engagement affects, not only the Bank of England, but the public who own the stock. The 'Loan Acts' contain a clause that 'all the Annuities aforesaid shall be payable and paid, and shall be transferable

c

at the Bank of England'; the holder of stock is therefore entitled to claim that the dividends shall continue to be paid at the Bank of England, and that he shall lose none of his securities, which he at present possesses, for their punctual payment, or the facilities afforded for the transfer of his stock.   Public faith would be shaken if any change were attempted which would in the slightest degree prejudice the interest of the stock-holder in these respects.   The arrangements which subsist between the Governor and the Bank of England for the payment of the dividends are framed with jealous care to insure punctuality in the discharge of this duty.   The advances by the Bank on deficiency bills, when the Government balances are insufficient for the purpose, insure the provision of the required funds; and although the Bank owes no direct responsibility to the stock-holder, and the National Debt stands on the credit of the State, the course of proceeding between the Government and the Bank, which is regulated by Parliament, affords an additional guarantee that money will be forthcoming for the payment of the dividends which could not subsist if the management were undertaken by a State Bank having no funds of its own to fall back upon. Were the Government so circumstanced it would be forced in case of a deficiency of funds to make terms with the banks, or resort to the open money market, instead of depending on an arrangement sanctioned by Parliament, and carried out by an Institution which owes a duty in this respect to the Government and the public. . . . It may be observed that the management of the National Debt as at present conducted by the Bank of England is not necessarily associated with its banking business. The transfer of stock is not immediately connected with the payment of money, and the dividends are discharged by warrants which are payable in a separate branch of the Bank. These operations might be conducted by a distinct establishment. . . . The 'Loan Acts,' however, require that the dividends should be actually paid at the Bank of England. This condition would not be fulfilled by an issue of dividend warrants payable at another establishment."

It is thus made manifest that this clause is the result of a jealous care to punctually discharge the payment of the dividends, and to literally fulfil the conditions on which the loans were obtained. Another clause provides that special officers shall be appointed for the fulfilment of these duties. So that instead of the "Loan Acts" creating any obligation on the part of the Government to preserve the Banking Department of the Bank of England, they make express provision against the contingency of its discontinuing its other business, by declaring it shall continue to be a Corporation for the purpose of paying the dividends; for the transfer of their stock; and for all other purposes of these Acts; until the whole of their claims are redeemed. The reference in the Treasury paper to the "duty" of the Banking Department of the Bank of England, in respect of making advances on deficiency bills to the Government and the public, must be understood to be in consequence of the consideration of the profits of the Bank as the bank of the Government. The principle on which the statement rests being that as the Bank sometimes makes a profit from utilising the deposits of the Government, so, on the other hand, it is only fair and just, and in conformity with banking practice, that it should be willing at other times to make advances to the Government should they be required.

We have now examined the various reasons
adduced in support of the contention that the
relations of the Banking Department of the
Bank of England with the Government place it
under some peculiar obligation to all other banks.
It will have been observed that in the case put
forward by Mr. R. C. L. Bevan, on behalf of the
other banks, it was not stated, in so many words,
that it is the " duty of the Bank of England to
keep money available at all times, to supply
the demands of bankers and others who have
rendered their own assets unavailable"; but the
claim that the Bank has no right to withhold
accommodation is equivalent to it, as, obviously,
the Bank could not grant the accommodation if
it did not keep cash in reserve for the purpose.
The claim as put forward then was unreasonable,
and there was nothing in the relations of the
Bank with the Government to sustain it. As
applied at the present time it is not only unreasonable and unjustifiable, but it is altogether
impracticable.   The Bank of England is no
longer the one Bank, towering above all its competitors, and able to control the rate of interest.
The operations of some of the joint-stock banks
are as extensive as those of the Bank of England;

and, collectively, the joint-stock banks arc the masters of the situation. So that the claim on the reserve of the Banking Department of the Bank of England, because of the relations of the Bank with the Government, must not only be abandoned as utterly unwarranted in principle; but also because it is absolutely impossible for the Bank—no longer exercising that commanding influence and power which in those days seemed to the other banks a reason for casting upon it extraordinary obligations — to practically fulfil the alleged " duty to keep money available at all times, to supply the demands of bankers who have rendered their own assets unavailable."

CHAPTER II.

THE ISSUE DEPARTMENT OF THE BANK OF ENGLAND.

THE only other important supply of available cash in this country than that of the Banking Department of the Bank of England, is kept by the Issue Department of the Bank of England; and in every crisis that has occurred since the separation of the Bank into two departments this reserve of cash has been made use of in order to supply the demands of bankers and others who had rendered their own assets unavailable. It is, therefore, obvious that the suspensions of the Bank Charter Act, 1844, lie at the root of the difficulty as to bank's cash reserves. If bankers may rely upon the reserve of bullion in the Issue Department being used as a basis on which to issue ready money in times of difficulty, it is not surprising if they do not incur the expense of keeping sufficient cash reserves of their own. It is not of vital importance to the Banking Department of the Bank of England whether its cash reserve is adequate or not, if it may, in an emergency, fall back upon the reserve of bullion in the

Issue Department; nor is it of supreme moment to the other banks whether the Banking Department of the Bank of England distinctly recognises and provides for their claim on its reserve, if, as is alleged, they can compel the Bank to supply them with ready money to the extent of its resources, and, if they are likely to prove insufficient, the Government can be relied upon to authorise the Bank to make use of the cash reserve of the Issue Department.

Ten years after the report of the Committee on Commercial Distress, 1847-8, referred to in the previous chapter, in which they assumed that the Banking Department of the Bank of England, in consequence of its relations with the Government, was under an obligation to supply the money-market with an unlimited quantity of ready money, another Committee was appointed to enquire into the circumstances which led to the suspension of the Act in 1857. This Committee, instead of basing the extraordinary claims on the Bank of England upon the relations of the Government with the Banking Department of the Bank of England, devoted its attention to the reserve in the Issue Department; and, quietly assuming the right of bankers and others, who

had rendered their own assets unavailable, to
make use of this reserve when required, took into
consideration the desirability, or otherwise, of
relaxing the provisions of the Bank Charter Act
1844, to enable them the more readily to do
so. Sec. 60 of their report states:—" The bank
directors say that the assistance which they gave
to the public would not have been ventured on
by them except for the Treasury letter (of the
12th Nov., 1857:—' If the directors of the Bank
of England should be unable in the present
emergency to meet the demands for discounts
and advances upon approved securities without
exceeding the limits of their circulation prescribed
by the Act of 1844, the Government will be prepared to propose to Parliament upon its meeting
a bill for any excess so issued '); nor would they
have ventured to act on that letter if the bullion
had been much lower than it was; for they must
have begun to think of the convertibility of the
note, which it would be their first duty to maintain; they attribute the maintenance of that
amount of bullion to the regulations provided by
the Act; and while they affirm that the present
court of directors having had more experience,
and having seen the gradual working of the Act

of 1844, would probably in their discretion have
adhered closely to the very regulations which the
Act required of them ; yet if they had not done
so, but had been induced to issue more than the
proportion which the law allowed, more gold
would have gone out by the action of the foreign
exchanges, and the consequences would have
been that they would have been left with less
gold as the panic came on ; and then, even with
the permission to issue more notes, they would
not have felt warranted in hazarding the circulation by doing so. They further state that for
these reasons it appears that the adoption of the
policy, which the Act now in force required,
placed the Bank of England in such a position
that it was enabled at the time of the severest
pressure to afford a larger aid to the commercial
public than would otherwise have been in their
power : that the true judgment of the court
would act in unison with the law; but yet it is
not expedient to expose them to the influence of
such a pressure as would inevitably be applied at
such a time; and that, upon the whole, with a
view to the operations of the Bank, including in
that category their being able to afford aid to
the commercial public at the time of severest

pressure, the Act of 1844 operated not as a fetter, but as a support decidedly. They therefore recommend that no relaxation should be made in the provisions of that law."

The apparent satisfaction with which the Committee regarded the breakdown of our monetary system as created by the Bank Charter Act of 1844, shows that they had not grasped the facts of the situation. The above section indicates that they were under the impression that the cash in the Issue Department had been specially set apart from the uses of the ordinary business of the Banking Department in order to form a reserve upon which the public might fall back in times of necessity. At any rate that seems to be the most reasonable construction to place upon the statement of the Bank directors, which the Committee apparently adopted, that the Act of 1844, "with a view to the operations of the Bank, including in that category their being able to afford aid to the commercial public at the time of the severest pressure, operated not as a fetter, but as a support decidedly." And in other sections of their report they labour to prove that the Act is never more thoroughly giving effect to those principles for the carrying out of which it was passed, than when its operations are suspended! Thus sec. 82, referring to the suspensions of the Act, states:—"Your Committee are satisfied to leave in the discretion of the executive government the time and prudent opportunity of giving further effect to those principles by which the convertibility of the Bank of England note has been kept above suspicion." In this way the Committee, whilst eulogising the Bank Charter Act 1844 for having kept the convertibility of the bank note above suspicion, assert that its suspension further effects that object!

One cannot help feeling a certain amount of sympathy for this Committee. They were placed in a very awkward dilemma. If they condemned the Bank Charter Act, 1844, and recommended a return to the old system of mixing up the business of banking with that of issuing notes, they were confronted with the declaration of the Bank directors that it was not expedient to expose them to the influence of such pressure as might hazard the circulation. On the other hand, if the Committee had consistently upheld the Act and had pointed out that the employment of the bullion in the Issue Department to supply

the money-market with ready money was to
divert it from its proper use, they would have
had reason to fear the consequences of the non-
suspension of the Act in future emergencies. It
does not seem to have occurred to them to point
out that the money-market's difficulties had arisen
from the overtrading of the banks in employing
too large a proportion of their funds, instead of
keeping adequate cash reserves. They, therefore, adopted a middle course. They decided to
recommend a continuance of the Act, but, at the
same time, to make provision for emergencies by
recommending that it should be suspended at the
discretion of the executive government. Unfortunately, however, they seem to have lacked the
courage to frankly state that such an anomaly
was the result of the force of circumstances; and,
instead of doing so, they endeavoured to justify
their recommendations by an appeal to the principles to give effect to which the Act had been
made law. In this they came hopelessly to grief,
and some portions of their report are simply
arrant nonsense. For example, compare sec. 66:
—"The main object of the legislation in question (the Bank Charter Act 1844) was undoubtedly to secure the variation of the paper

currency of the kingdom according to the same laws by which a metallic circulation would vary. No one contends that this object has not been obtained"; with sec. 72, " Your committee think that such a provision (for increasing the number of notes in times of pressure, irrespective of a corresponding deposit of bullion) could not be regarded as any violation of the principle of the Act of 1844." If the principle of the Act were to secure the variation of the paper currency according to the same laws by which a metallic currency would vary (which has been effected by only permitting the issue of paper over and above a certain amount, below which experience had shown the amount of circulation did not go, upon the deposit of bullion, and enforcing cash payments on presentation) it is simply absurd to allege that that principle would not be violated by an extra issue of paper without the metal.

The Committee were not more fortunate in their references to the speeches of the authors of the Act than they were in their appeal to its abstract principles. Sec. 71, " It is here neces- sary for the Committee to advert to the question whether the law should be left, subject only to that power which was contemplated by Sir Robert .

Peel and Mr. Huskisson, and was actually exercised by the two governments of 1847 and 1857; or, on the other hand, provision should be made in advance for such contingencies, and the conditions expressly laid down on which the issue of an increased number of bank notes may in the time of pressure be allowed." Sec. 72:—"Your Committee think such a provision could not be regarded as any violation of the principle of the Act of 1844. To have introduced such an express provision when the law itself was first adopted by Parliament, or even when as in 1848 it had only been a few years in operation, and was comparatively little understood, was a far more serious question of policy and prudence than it can in fairness be regarded at the present time. Yet the interference of the Government in an extreme case, must in fact be taken to have been contemplated by the framers of the Act. Mr. Cotton stated to the Committee of 1847-8 that this subject was considered when the Act was in preparation in 1844, and that Sir Robert Peel's opinion was thus expressed:—' If it be necessary to assume a grave responsibility, I daresay men will be found willing to assume such responsibility.' It scarcely, therefore, con-

stitutes of itself a sufficient ground for bringing
this important and difficult subject under the
review of Parliament, and may properly
await the decision of the legislature when the
other branches of the subject shall be dealt
with."

There is all the difference in the world between
Sir Robert Peel's statement that if it be necessary
to assume a grave responsibility men would be
found willing to assume such responsibility, and
the Committee's report deliberately approving of
the suspensions of the Act, and maintaining that
the authors had always intended that it should
be suspended from time to time. After the first
suspension of the Act, Sir Robert Peel, speaking
in the House of Commons on the 3rd Dec., 1847
(Hansard, p. 668), expressed his approval of the
action of the Government as follows :—" But
when there occurs a state of panic—a state of
things which cannot be foreseen, or provided
against by law—which cannot be reasoned with,
the Government must assume a power to prevent
the consequences which may occur. There is a
necessity for a discretion which I think was
properly exercised in the present instance. It
was better to authorise a violation of the law

than to run the risk of the consequences which might have ensued if no intervention on the part of the Government had taken place." Mr. Glyn, speaking ten years afterwards, gave his opinion of the necessity of the suspension of the Act in 1857 in very forcible language. He said (3 Hansard cxlviii., p. 187, Dec. 4th, 1857) :— " It was reduced to a simple matter of fact that when a time of pressure came a letter, or some such instrument, must be issued to relieve the Act of 1844, and he hoped that the Government of this country would never fall into the hands of any individual hardy enough to carry out what were called the first principles of the Act. If any person should attempt to do so he would speedily be hurled from power, not by any vote of the House, but by the physical power of the country. (Oh). That statement seemed to give rise to some difference of opinion, but did hon. members who cried 'Oh' suppose that all the people connected with the mill power of this country, with the mining interests, that the mass of operatives thrown out of employment would be content to remain without wages or means of existence simply because a principle, so called, was to be maintained ? Therefore he did not

D

believe any public man would attempt to uphold the Act under those circumstances." These are very definite and cogent reasons which rendered the suspension of the Act a dire necessity. But they are very different from the Committee's futile attempt to represent that the authors of the Act anticipated its suspension with approval. Sir Robert Peel recognised that the Government had to choose between two evils, and of the two "it was better to authorise a violation of the law than to run the risk of the consequences which might have ensued if no intervention on the part of the Government had taken place." And not only did he speak of the suspension of the Act as a "violation of the law," he also referred to it as a tampering with the standard of value (p. 665) : " When I see the insolvency of a house of which the liabilities amount to £50,000, and the assets to £3,000, I cannot but say that if that be the practice of your commerce then do not complain of the Act of 1844, or of any other measure, as the cause of your embarrassments. I ask is it not monstrous that the standard of value in this country should be tampered with in order to facilitate and uphold such transactions as these ? "

In the face of these quotations from Sir Robert Peel's speech after the suspension of the Act, what is the value of the expression to which he gave utterance before the passing of the Act to the effect that " if it be necessary to assume a grave responsibility, I daresay men will be found willing to assume such responsibility?" He regarded the suspension of the Act as a breakdown of our financial system: it was a "violation of the law," and a " tampering with the standard of value."

In some quarters, however, the violation of the law in 1857 was not regarded with the same equanimity as the Committee displayed. The Chancellor of the Exchequer (Sir Geo. Cornewall Lewis) said (Hansard, 4th Dec., 1857, p. 162). " It has been said that the Government have authorised the Bank to commit an act equivalent to a depreciation of the currency ; that what we have done amounted almost to permitting the repudiation of contracts ; that the sanctity of property was invaded by this additional issue of bank notes. I entirely dispute the correctness of that view. The additional notes issued by the Bank, under our authority, were like other notes payable on demand; if any doubt had arisen as to their instantaneous convertibility there would have been some ground for the charge which has been made against the Government. All we said to the Bank was that whereas the original limit of notes based on securities was 14 millions, increased by an order in council to £14,475,000, they might for a limited time, and for a limited object, increase the issue of that class. But inasmuch as the additional issue by the Bank was not sufficient to affect the value of the notes, and each note was convertible into gold upon demand, it cannot be said, with justice, that the Government have depreciated the currency, authorised a repudiation of contracts, or struck at the security and sanctity of property."

This reply of the Chancellor of the Exchequer, however, scarcely meets the case. The intrenchment upon the security given to the holders of bank notes for their convertibility consisted of the power given to the Bank of England to increase the number of claims upon the bullion. As the proportion of notes issued against securities to those issued against bullion was increased beyond the amount laid down in the Act so the security given for the convertibility of the notes was diminished. And the reply that the security was so good that it was diminished without risk, does not answer the charge of having authorised a repudiation of contract. The condonation of the suspensions of the Act rests upon the desirability of choosing the lesser of two evils, and it is a false policy to deny that the lesser was an evil at all. Had the evil been fairly recognised some attempt might have been made to avoid it in the future. It is, therefore, very important not to minimise the consequences of the violations of the law, and there can be no doubt that in weakening the security for the convertibility on demand of the note the Government did commit a breach of contract with the note holders.

The late Mr. J. W. Gilbart, who was one of the directors of the London and Westminster Bank, and previously general manager, has, however, suggested a very ingenious way of regarding the security given for the convertibility of Bank of England notes. In the " Principles and practice of banking," p. 231—Edition 1873, he says :—" By the phrase ' securing the convertibility of the note,' it is not meant that the Issue Department of the Bank of England held a sufficient amount of gold and silver to pay off all the notes it had issued. It is obvious that the

gold and silver in hand must always be fourteen
millions less than this amount, inasmuch as fourteen millions of notes are issued against securities.
By ' securing the convertibility of the note,' is
meant that the Issue Department of the Bank of
England were in a condition to pay off any
amount of notes of which payment was likely to
be demanded *for the purpose of exporting gold*—the
Issue Department was always in a. condition to
meet any foreign demand for gold.   This is called
' securing the convertibility of the notes.' "

It will be seen that Mr. Gilbart's view of the
phrase " securing the convertibility of the note,"
strikingly contrasts with that of Sir George
Cornewall Lewis, who, as quoted above, declared
that notwithstanding the suspension of the Act in
1857 as " each note was convertible upon demand
it could not be said that the Government had
depreciated the currency, authorised a repudiation
of contracts, or struck at the security and sanctity
of property."   Nor was it the view of Sir Robert
Peel.   On the 6th Jan., 1844, in reply to a
question of Mr. Muntz who " wished to know
what would happen in consequence of there being
such an export of gold as would render it impossible for the Bank to pay its liabilities in

gold ?" Sir Robert Peel said, "The intention
undoubtedly was that any demand on the Bank
of England would be paid in gold if desired. It
would have the power of issuing notes to the
amount of fourteen millions on securities, and
might diminish that issue to eleven millions, the
amount of the Government debt, if it should be
necessary. The Bank had the complete control
over the three millions, but if the eleven millions
of Government debt should be required by the
Bank, the Government would have no difficulty
in raising the amount to pay it off. He, however, by no means anticipated such a contingency
as that which had entered into the speculative
mind of the hon. gentleman. He could only
repeat that all demands on the Bank must, if
desired, be paid in gold." After the suspension
of the Act in 1847, a suggestion was made that
the debt of the Government might be paid with
inconvertible paper which he repudiated as
follows (3 Hansard xcv., 669-70, Dec. 3rd,
1847):—"I think I heard from the hon. member
for Wakefield last night a recommendation that
the Government should pay off its debt of fourteen millions to the Bank, and should pay it in
inconvertible paper. Sir, if the Government is

to set the example of paying its debts in inconvertible paper—in paper for which there is no other equivalent than some other paper— if that is to be the example set by the Government, I daresay that individuals in a similar difficulty will be glad to profit by that example. But I cannot believe that this House will sanction such an injustice as that the Government shall pay the Bank the amount of a public debt in inconvertible paper."

It is evident from these speeches that Sir Robert Peel intended that the "securities" against which a portion of the notes are issued should be capable of realisation, and there is, therefore, no warrant for Mr. Gilbart's assertion, that only those notes of which payment was likely to be demanded for the export of gold were meant to be convertible.

The Act* says, *inter alia*—

I.—"That from and after the 31st August, 1844, the issue of promissory notes of the Governor and Co. of the Bank of England, payable on demand, shall be kept wholly distinct

* NOTE.—In Appendix A is a paper dealing with the legal aspect, prepared by Mr. Freshfield; but it is so clearly a one-sided document that it has not seemed necessary to insert it here.

from the general banking business of the said
Governor, etc.; and the business of such issue
shall be thenceforth conducted and carried on by
the said Governor and Co. in a separate department to be called ' the Issue Department of the
Bank of England.'

II.—" That upon the same day there shall be
transferred, appropriated, and set apart by the
said Governor and Co. to the Issue Department,
securities to the value of £14,000,000, whereof
the debt due by the public to the said Governor and Co. shall be a part; and at the same
time so much of the gold coin, and gold and
silver bullion as shall not be required by the
Banking Department; and, thereupon, there shall
be delivered out of the Issue Department into
the Banking Department such an amount of
notes as, together with the notes then in circulation, shall be equal to the aggregate amount of
the securities, coin and bullion so transferred to
to the Issue Department; and the whole amount
of Bank of England notes then in circulation,
including those delivered to the Banking Department as aforesaid, shall be deemed to be issued
on the credit of such securities, coin and bullion
so appropriated and set apart to the Issue Depart-

ment; and it shall not be lawful for the Governor
and Co. to increase the amount of securities
(except in the case of other banks ceasing to
issue, when it shall be lawful for Her Majesty in
Council to authorise an increase of not exceeding
two-thirds of the amount, which the bankers so
ceasing may have been authorised to issue), but
it shall be lawful for them to diminish the amount
of such securities, and again to increase the same
to any sum not exceeding in the whole the sum
of £14,000,000, and so on from time to time as
they shall see occasion ; and from and after such
transfer and appropriation to the Issue Department it shall not be lawful for the Governor and
Co. to issue bank notes, either into the Banking
Department, or to any persons or person what-
soever, save in exchange for other Bank of
England notes, or for gold coin or for gold or
silver bullion, received or purchased for the Issue
Department under the provisions of this Act, or
in exchange for securities acquired and taken in
the Issue Department under its provision : provided always that it shall be lawful for the said
Governor and Co. in their Banking Department
to issue all such Bank of England Notes as they
shall at any time receive from the said Issue

Department or otherwise, in the same manner in all respects as such issue would be lawful to any other person or persons."

Now it is not a little curious that Mr. Gilbart in stating the principal provisions of the Act in his "Principles and Practice of Banking" has omitted the following words in sec. 2, quoted above:—"And the whole amount of Bank of England notes then in circulation, including those delivered to the Banking Department as aforesaid, shall be deemed to be issued on the credit of such securities, coin and bullion so appropriated and set apart to the Issue Department." Having satisfied himself that the promises of all the notes to pay on demand were not intended to be fulfilled, he probably did not consider it of importance to state the particulars of the security appropriated and set apart for their payment. Nevertheless it will be seen that every care has been taken to render the convertibility of all the Bank of England notes above suspicion. The first clause, quoted above, entirely separates the business of issue from the ordinary banking business of the Bank of England and provides that it shall be carried on in a separate department. The second clause

definitely fixes the amount which shall be issued
upon certain securities, appropriated and set
apart for the purpose at such a moderate sum
that the average proportion of the notes issued
against gold to those issued against securities
for the first year after the Act came into operation was over 90 per cent., and it has never been
below 70 per cent. in any year since. In fact,
the Act has made the Issue Department of the
Bank of England, to all intents and purposes,
a national institution; created for the administration of a national currency; with the directors
of the Bank of England appointed, as officials *
of the Government, to administer its affairs upon
strict lines from which they have no power to
depart.

The mere fact that the directors of the Bank
of England are managers on behalf of the public
of the circulation of the country, under regulations which give them no more facilities to obtain
the legal tender for carrying on their banking
business than have the directors of any other

---

* Note.—The Chancellor of the Exchequer writing to the Governor
and Deputy Governor of the Bank of England on 26th April, 1844,
says : " In fixing the proportion of the amount which ought to be paid
to the public I do not, on the one hand, put out of view the fair claim
of the Bank to compensation *as managers on behalf of the public of the
circulation of the country.*

bank, affords no justification for a reliance upon
the reserve in the Issue Department. That
reserve has been appropriated, and set apart,
to secure the convertibility of the bank notes;
and cannot properly be regarded as money available at all times to supply the demands of
bankers and others who have rendered their
own assets unavailable.

The effect, however, of the three suspensions
of the Act has been so completely to imbue "the
City mind" with the idea that the bullion in the
Issue Department may be utilised in an emergency for the purpose of increasing the money-
market's supply of available cash that on the
occasion of the recent "Baring Crisis" it is
generally understood that the Directors of the
Bank of England actually made arrangements
with the Government—and obtained their consent—for the suspension of the Act before the
firm's difficulties became known to the public.
The adoption of this policy prevented a great
disaster; but it was tantamount to an admission
that the cash reserves of the banks were not
equal to the strain which a failure of that magnitude might have occasioned.

Under these circumstances it is not surprising

that Mr. Goschen feels the time has come when the question of banks' cash reserves should be dealt with. It is a serious matter that the Government should have again been called upon to authorise a violation of the law; and that the security for the convertibility of the notes, created by Act of Parliament, should be impaired under any stress of circumstances. The three actual suspensions of the Act have, moreover, involved a great hardship upon those who happened to succumb just before the suspensions took place, and who would have surmounted their difficulties if they had taken place earlier. The arbitrary interference with the law of the country just in time to save A who had to meet liabilities on Tuesday, whilst B whose liabilities became due on Monday was allowed to fail, is a very invidious act, and condemns the system which necessitates it.

CHAPTER III.

"LOMBARD STREET."

MR. BAGEHOT in his " Lombard Street " does not base the claim upon the Bank of England to keep a reserve for the purpose of supplying the demands of bankers and others when they have rendered their own assets unavailable, upon the relations of the Government either with the Banking Department or the Issue Department. He says (p. 63) :—" It is imagined that because bank notes are a legal tender, the Bank has some peculiar duty to help other people. But bank notes are only a legal tender at the Issue Department, not at the Banking Department, and the accidental combination of the two departments in the same building gives the Banking Department no aid in meeting a panic. If the Issue Department were at Somerset House, and if it issued Government notes there, the position of the Banking Department under the present law would be exactly what it is now. No doubt, formerly, the Bank of England could

issue what it pleased, but that historical remi-
niscence makes it no stronger now that it can
no longer so issue. We must deal with what
is, not with what was. And a still worse argument is also used. It is said that because the
Bank of England keeps the 'State account,'
and is the Government banker, it is a sort of
'public institution' and ought to help everybody. But the custody of the taxes which have
been collected and which wait to be expended
is a duty quite apart from panics. The Government money may chance to be much or little
when the panic comes. There is no relation or
connection between the two. And the State
in getting the Bank to keep what money it may
chance to have, or in borrowing of it what it
may chance to want, does not hire it to stop a
panic or much help it if it tries."

In this way he throws overboard the reasons
which had been previously given for the extraordinary assertion that it is the Bank of England's duty to save all other banks the trouble
and expense of keeping cash reserves. Nevertheless he reiterates the demand, declaring that
hitherto (p. 63) " the real reason has not been
distinctly seen." Under these circumstances

he appears somewhat inconsistent in expressing surprise—notwithstanding the fact that the real reason had not been distinctly seen—that the recognition of this " duty " had not been enforced by Parliament. He says (p. 41):—" It might be expected that as this great public duty was cast upon the Banking Department of the Bank, the principal statesmen (if not Parliament itself) would have enjoined on them to perform it. But no distinct resolution of Parliament has ever enjoined it; scarcely any stray word of any influential statesman. And on the contrary, there is a whole *catena* of authorities, beginning with Sir Robert Peel and ending with Mr. Lowe, which say that the Banking Department of the Bank of England is only a Bank like any other bank—a Company like other companies; that in this capacity it has no peculiar position and no public duties at all." Again on p. 62:— " We are apt to be solemnly told that the Banking Department of the Bank of England is only a Bank like other banks—that it has no peculiar duty in times of panic—that it then is to look to itself alone, as other banks look. And there is this excuse for the Bank. Hitherto questions of banking have been so little dis-

E

cussed in comparison with questions of currency
that the duty of the Bank in time of panic has
been put on a wrong ground.

The " real reason" why the Bank is not like
other banks is explained on p. 35. After showing that when a run takes place the bullion to
meet it must be taken from the Bank of England
as there is no other large store in the country,
he says :—" In consequence all. our credit
system depends on the Bank of England for its
security. On the wisdom of the directors of
that one Joint-Stock Company, it depends
whether *England shall be solvent or insolvent.*
This may seem too strong, but it is not. All
banks depend on the Bank of England, and all
merchants depend on some banker. If a merchant have £10,000 at his bankers, and wants
to pay someone in Germany, he will not be able
to pay it unless his banker can pay him, and
the banker will not be able to pay if the Bank
of England should be in difficulties and cannot
produce his 'reserve.' The Directors of the
Bank are, therefore, in fact, if not in name,
trustees for the public, to keep a banking reserve
on their behalf; and it would naturally be expected either that they distinctly recognised

this duty and engaged to perform it, or that their own self-interest was so strong in the matter that no engagement was needed. But so far from their being a distinct undertaking on the part of the Bank directors to perform this duty, many of them would scarcely acknowledge it, and some altogether deny it."

Now it will be observed that the whole of this argument is founded upon a consideration of the consequences which would ensue if the Bank of England was in difficulties and could not produce the " reserve " of the other bank—in other words, if the Bank of England could not repay the balance standing to the credit of the other bank. But the conclusion that there is no distinct undertaking on the part of the Bank of England to keep a reserve for this purpose, and that some of the directors would scarcely acknowledge it as a duty, and some " altogether deny it," is plainly erroneous, for that would amount to a denial that the Bank of England undertakes to pay its liabilities in cash. Of course if in the hypothetical case, which "Lombard Street" furnishes, the amount of the bank's reserve with the Bank of England was £10,000, the bank would have an undoubted right to demand it. But the illustration will not sustain the conclusion that it is the duty of the Bank of England to keep a reserve for any other purpose than to meet the claims of its depositors; and it cannot, therefore, be regarded as relevant to the controversy.

To more accurately represent the point at issue the case should have been thus stated :— "If a merchant have £10,000 at his bankers and wants to pay someone in Germany, he will not be able to pay it unless his banker can pay him, and the banker will not be able to pay if the amount of his reserve at the Bank of England is not equal to the amount required, and the Bank of England refuses to make an advance." The whole gist of the controversy turns upon the alleged " duty " of the Bank of England to "keep money available at all times to supply the demands of bankers who have rendered their own assets unavailable," and to attempt to prove this by an illustration which assumes that no advance is required from the Bank of England is to beg the question.

' Lombard Street ' also explains the ' real reason ' why the Bank of England should save other banks the trouble and expense of keeping

cash reserves of their own as follows (p. 63) :—
" As has been already said—but on account of
its importance and perhaps its novelty it is
worth saying again—whatever bank or banks
keep the ultimate banking reserve of the country
must lend that reserve most freely in time of
apprehension, for that is one of the characteristic
uses of the bank reserve, and the mode in which
it attains one of the main ends for which it is
kept. Whether rightly or wrongly, at present
and in fact the Bank of England keeps our
ultimate bank reserve, and therefore it must use
it in this manner." On p. 65 :—" The holders
of the bank reserve ought to lend at once, and
most freely in an incipient panic, because they
fear destruction in the panic. They ought not
to do it to save others ; they ought to do it to
save themselves. They ought to know that this
bold policy is the only safe one, and for that
reason they ought to choose it." Again on
p. 187 :—" The Bank of England is bound
according to our system, not only to keep a
good reserve against a time of panic, but to use
that reserve effectually when that time of panic
comes. The keepers of the bank reserve, whether
one or many, are obliged then to use that reserve

for their own safety. If they permit all other
forms to perish, their own will perish immediately,
and in consequence."

This argument is the converse of the one
previously considered. Here it is not the Bank
of England in difficulties rendering all others
insolvent, but all other forms of credit perish-
ing are threatening the safety of the Bank of
England. As a matter of policy there can be
no doubt that at such a time as Mr. Bagehot
describes, the Bank of England should try its
only chance of safety. But the case is not
merely advanced in order to represent the only
course open to the Bank when those circumstances actually arose : it is employed in support
of an alleged ' duty '—directly in the interest
of the Bank, but indirectly for the benefit of
others—in anticipation of those events. To
syllogise the argument it would stand thus :—

The Bank of England must perish if all other forms
of credit do.

All other forms of credit must perish if the Bank of
England does not keep a reserve out of which to make
unlimited advances on securities to anyone who applies
for them.

Therefore the Bank of England ought (for its own
safety) to keep a reserve out of which to make unlimited
advances on securities to anyone who applies for them.

Thus the axiom of the argument is the un-doubted ' duty ' of the Bank of England to preserve its own safety. But it does not seem to have occurred to Mr. Bagehot that it is equally the undoubted duty of every other bank to preserve itself from destruction ; and that it would be more equitable, instead of making a scapegoat of the Bank of England—which it is assumed would hold out the longest—to make each bank bear its own burden.

" Lombard Street" is not more just to the Bank of England when it compares the reserve of that Institution with those of its competitors, than in its attempt to saddle the Bank of England with the responsibility of keeping a supply of ready money to supply their deficiencies in time of need. On p. 39 it says :—" In most banks there would be a wholesome dread re-straining the desire of the shareholders to reduce the reserve ; they would fear to impair the credit of the bank. But fortunately or unfortunately no one has any fear about the Bank of England. The English world at least believes that it will not, almost that it *cannot*, fail. Three times since 1844 the Banking Department has received assistance, and would have failed without it.

In 1825 the entire concern almost suspended payment; in 1797, it actually did so. But still there is a faith in the Bank, contrary to experience, and despising evidence. No doubt in every one of these years the condition of the Bank, divided or undivided, was in a certain sense most sound; it could *ultimately* have paid all its creditors all it owed, and returned to its shareholders all their own capital. But ultimate payment is not what the creditors of a bank want; they want present, not postponed, payment; they want to be repaid according to agreement: the contract was that they should be paid on demand, and if they are not paid on demand they may be ruined. And that instant payment, in the years I speak of, the Bank of England certainly could not have made. But no one in London ever dreams of questioning the credit of the Bank, and the Bank never dreams that its own credit is in danger. Somehow everybody feels the Bank is sure to come right. In 1797 when it had scarcely any money left, the Government said not only that it need not pay away what remained, but that it *must* not. The ' effect of letters of licence ' to break Peel's Act has confirmed the popular conviction that the Government is close behind the Bank, and will help it when wanted. Neither the Bank nor the Banking Department have ever had an idea of being put 'into liquidation'; most men would think as soon of 'winding up' the English nation. Since then the Bank of England, as a bank, is exempted from the perpetual apprehension that makes other bankers keep a large reserve—the apprehension of discredit—it would seem particularly necessary that its managers should be themselves specially interested in keeping that reserve, and specially competent to keep it."

Anyone who did not know the facts with regard to the reserves kept by the Bank of England, and the other banks respectively, would suppose, after reading the above, that the Bank of England kept a much smaller reserve than the other banks: that it did so because it did not share that "wholesome dread restraining the desire of the shareholders to reduce the reserve," the "fear to impair the credit of the Bank"; that being "exempted from the perpetual apprehension that makes other bankers keep a large reserve—the apprehension of discredit"—it had no sufficient motive to keep so large a reserve.

Nothing could be more contrary to the fact. And what renders this attack upon the Bank of England most extraordinary is, that it was only on the previous page (38) that he was comparing the amount of the reserve kept by that Institution with the reserves of the other banks, and pointing out the loss which the proprietors of the Bank sustained because of the much larger reserve which it kept. He says:—" Some part of the lowness of the Bank dividend, and of the consequent small value of Bank stock, is undoubtedly caused by the magnitude of the Bank capital; but much of it is also due to the great amount of unproductive cash—of cash which yields no interest—that the Banking Department of the Bank of England keeps lying idle. If we compare the London and Westminster Bank—which is the first of the joint-stock banks in the public estimation and known to be very cautiously and carefully managed—with the Bank of England, we shall see the difference at once. The London and Westminster has only 13 per cent. of its liabilities lying idle. The Banking Department of the Bank of England has over 40 per cent."

Thus, the statement that the Bank of England is " exempted from the perpetual apprehension

that makes other bankers keep a large reserve—
the apprehension of discredit" is not borne out
by the fact, that the London and Westminster
Bank has only 13 per cent. of its liabilities lying
idle, whilst the Banking Department of the Bank
of England has over 40 per cent. But then
"Lombard Street" has a very peculiar way of
referring to the relative proportions of the reserves
of the Bank of England and the other banks. In
another place, the fact that the Bank of England
keeps a larger reserve than the other banks is
employed to support the claim on the Bank to
keep a reserve to supply their deficiencies, thus
p. 35:—"So far from there being a distinct
undertaking on the part of the Bank directors to
perform this duty (of keeping a banking reserve
on behalf of the public) many of them would
scarcely acknowledge it, and some altogether
deny it. Mr. Hankey, one of the most careful
and most experienced of them, says in his book
on the Bank of England:—I do not intend here
to enter at any length on the subject of the
general management of the Bank, meaning the
Banking Department, as the principle upon which
the business is conducted does not differ, as far
as I am aware, from that of any well-conducted

bank in London." But as anyone can see by the published figures, the Banking Department of the Bank of England keeps as a great reserve in bank notes and coin between 30 and 50 per cent. of its liabilities, and the other banks only keep in bank notes and coin the bare minimum they need to open shop with. And such a constant difference indicates, I conceive, that the two are *not* managed on the same principle."

In this case the London and Westminster Bank is not to get the benefit of the 13 per cent. of its liabilities lying idle, "the other banks only keep in bank notes and coin the bare minimum they need to open shop with." Its reserve (or balance) at the Bank is not to count. Why? The published figures of the London and Westminster Bank show that it treats its balance at the Bank as cash, and consequently in any argument as to the principle upon which that bank manages its business it cannot be ignored. However, on another page (171) "Lombard Street," admits this balance at the Bank as a factor in the argument:—"Mr. Hankey should have observed that we know by the published figures that the joint-stock banks in London do not keep one-third, or anything like one-third, of their liabilities in 'cash'—even meaning by 'cash' a deposit at the Bank of England. One third of the deposits in joint-stock banks, not to speak of the private banks would be £30,000,000; and the private deposits of the Bank of England are £18,000,000. According to his own statement, there is a conspicuous contrast. The joint-stock banks, and the private banks, no doubt, too, keep one sort of reserve, and the Bank of England a different kind of reserve altogether. Mr. Hankey says the two ought to be managed on the same principle; but if so he should have said whether he would assimilate the practice of the Bank of England, to that of the other Banks, or that of the other banks, to the practice of the Bank of England."

The answer to this question does not seem far to seek. Mr. Hankey had said p. 169 :—" The 'Economist' newspaper has put forth what in my opinion is the most mischievous doctrine ever broached in the monetary or banking world in this country, viz.:—that it is the proper function of the Bank of England to keep money available at all times to supply the demands of bankers who have rendered their own assets unavailable. Until such a doctrine is repudiated by the banking

interest, the difficulty of pursuing any sound
principle of banking in London will be always
very great. But I do not believe that such a
doctrine as that bankers are justified in relying
on the Bank of England to assist them in time of
need is generally held by the bankers in London."
Thus the principle upon which Mr. Hankey contends that both the Bank of England and the
joint-stock banks should be managed is, clearly,
a reliance upon their own resources. The fact
that the London and Westminster Bank only
keeps a reserve against liabilities of 13 per cent.
as compared with the 40 per cent. kept by the
Bank of England does not necessarily imply that
the former is relying upon the latter in times
of difficulty. The nature of their respective liabilities must be considered. To begin with, nearly
all the liabilities of the Bank of England are
payable on demand, whereas the London and
Westminster receives money on interest, not
repayable until after notice. But if " Lombard
Street " assumes that the much smaller proportion
of reserve to liabilities, kept by the London and
Westminster Bank indicates that the directors are
relying upon the Bank of England in time of
need, undoubtedly Mr. Hankey would assimilate

the practice of the London and Westminster to
the practice of the Bank of England, and insist
that it ought to keep a sufficient reserve with
which to supply its own requirements on a rainy
day. If it does not, it ought to. It would be
monstrously unjust to allege that the fact of its
not doing so would render it incumbent upon the
Bank of England to keep such a reserve for it.
But something of the sort seems to be implied
in the following extract from " Lombard Street,"
p. 171:—"Mr. Hankey should have shown 'some
other store of unused cash' except the reserve
in the Banking Department of the Bank of England out of which advances in time of panic could
be made. These advances are necessary, and
must be made by someone. The 'reserves' of
London bankers are not such store, they are *used*
cash, not unused; they are part of the Bank
deposits, and lent as such." The fallacy in this
argument lies in the assumption that in times
of panic the Bank of England is the only bank
that can make advances, since the reserves of the
other banks are "locked up" and cannot be made
use of. But what is to prevent any of the other
banks utilising the money standing to their credit
at the Bank? If it is said that the Bank could

not produce it, then it follows that the Bank would not be in a position to make the "advances which are necessary, and must be made by some-one." The same fallacy lies at the root of another of " Lombard Street's " replies to Mr. Hankey. On p. 172 : " Mr. Hankey should have observed that, as has been explained, in most panics, the principal use of a ' banking reserve ' is not to advance to bankers ; the largest amount is almost always advanced to the mercantile public and to bill-brokers. But the point is that by our system all extra pressure is thrown upon the Bank of England. In the worst part of the crisis of 1866, £50,000 ' fresh money' could not be borrowed, even on the best security—even on Consols—except at the Bank of England. There was no other lender to new borrowers." The fact that the Bank of England, in the crisis of 1866, was the only lender to new borrowers, is a very extraordinary reason to give why it should for ever after be the only Bank whose sole "duty" it is to keep a supply of ready money in order to do so in the future. But here again there is the erroneous assumption that the other banks could not lend on Consols. They could have done so if they had chosen. As

" Lombard Street " says (p. 315): " In a panic the
bankers' balances greatly augment," why should
they not have been employed? If the Bank had
fresh money to lend, the other banks who had
balances at the Bank could have used that money.
It is not the fault of our system that " all extra
pressure is thrown upon the Bank of England";
it is because other banks, fearing that their reserves
are not sufficient to enable them to meet the extra
demands that may then be made upon them,
commence to hoard their resources, and to decline
to grant the accommodation they had previously
given. If we had a many-reserve system, instead
of a one-reserve system, and the banks had the
same amount in their own coffers as they had at
the Bank of England, and they adopted the same
policy of restricting their advances in times of panic,
all the extra pressure would still be thrown upon
the Bank of England. It is not a question of one
reserve or many reserves: it is a question whether
they are sufficient to enable the respective banks
to take their fair share of responsibility in times
of pressure. This Mr. Hankey said the Bank of
England was prepared to do (p. 170): " I consider it to be the undoubted duty of the Bank of
England to hold its banking deposits (reserving

F

generally about one-third in cash) in the most available securities; and in the event of a sudden pressure in the money market, by whatever circumstance it may be caused, to bear its full share of a drain on its resources." To which "Lombard St." objects that (p. 173): "His words are too vague. No one can tell what a fair share means; still less can we tell what other people at some future time will say it means. Theory suggests, and experience proves, that in a panic the holders of the ultimate Bank reserve (whether one bank or many) should lend to all that bring good securities, quickly, freely, and readily. By that policy they allay a panic; by every other policy they intensify it. The public have a right to know whether the Bank of England—the holders of our ultimate bank reserve—acknowledge this duty, and are ready to perform it. But this is now very uncertain." Unquestionably, in a time of panic, a bold policy is a safe policy; but it is not to be confined to the Bank of England. The other banks should be prepared to take their share of a drain on their resources. The fact that the reserve of the Bank of England is in its own custody, and that the other banks keep their reserves at the Bank of England, makes no difference in the policy

which should be adopted by them all. Before
the drain takes place they should have reserves
corresponding to their liabilities, which they could
afford to see substantially reduced without having
to restrict their ordinary advances. But when a
bank has been trading up to the hilt, and a drain
commences, and it is obliged to meet it by restricting its ordinary advances, it does not bear its
fair share of responsibility; on the contrary, by
declining to grant the usual facilities, it creates a
sense of uneasiness, and thereby intensifies the
panic. Whether the banks keep their reserves at
the Bank of England, or in their own vaults, is a
matter for them to elect ; but wherever they are
kept, they should be adequate to supply their own
needs in times of difficulty, as they have no right
to expect " the Bank of England to keep money
available at all times, to supply the demands of
bankers who have rendered their own assets unavailable."

The foregoing are all the arguments employed
by "Lombard Street" to prove its case. In replying
to them it has not been necessary to express any
opinion on the advantage, or disadvantage, of a
one, or a many, reserve system. If the other
banks consider that the present system has failed

it is within their power to alter it. They have a right to expect the Bank to keep itself in a position to repay their balances; and if they are not satisfied with the way in which it fulfils its duty in this respect, they can withdraw them, and either keep them under their own individual control, or create a general fund to be administered by their representatives. But none of the reasons supplied by " Lombard St." justify them in relying upon the Bank of England to save all other banks the trouble and expense of keeping cash reserves of their own.

CHAPTER IV.

CASH RESERVES.

THE first time the reserves of the banks were brought under the public notice appears to have been in 1856, in a letter by Mr. Weguelin, the Governor of the Bank of England, to Sir George Cornewall Lewis, the Chancellor of the Exchequer. Mr. Weguelin wrote:—

" If the amount of the reserve kept by the Bank of England be contrasted with the reserve kept by the joint-stock banks, a new and hitherto little considered source of danger to the credit of the country will present itself. The joint-stock banks of London, judging by their published accounts, have deposits to the amount of £30,000,000. Their capital is not more than £3,000,000, and they have on an average £31,000,000 invested in one way or another, leaving only £2,000,000 as reserve against all this mass of liabilities. It is impossible to foresee the consequences of the failure of one of these large establishments, and it is a branch of the subject which, in my opinion, more pressingly requires the attention of Parliament than any alteration in the Banking Acts of 1844 and 1845."

This portion of Mr. Weguelin's letter does not appear to have attracted the attention it deserved, for as Mr. Bagehot observes, "the air was obscured by other matters," the discussion at that period being confined to the operation of the Bank Charter Act, 1844. Since then the importance of the matter has considerably increased, and Mr. Goschen referred to it at Leeds on the 28th Jan. last as follows:—

"I come now to a point of scarcely less interest (than the suggested issue of £1 notes), and that is the reserves of the country, apart from the question of gold, and there I must give utterance to a strong conviction which I hold, that the banking reserves of the country are inadequate to the necessities of the country and are too small as compared with the gigantic liabilities which our large institutions have incurred. On that point I should wish to put a figure or two before you. They are stupendous figures. Ordinary mortals are unable to understand astronomers when they tell us the distance in miles which we are from the sun, and ordinary mortals can scarcely grasp the hundreds of millions which enter into the transactions of our great joint-stock banks. I wish to put this argument before you—that in times of crises reserves are essential, and that it is of supreme importance that all the great banks of the country, at the moment a crisis comes, should be able to afford relief to their customers rather than feel at that moment bound to curtail the facilities which they are giving. It is all very well for banks to give facilities to their customers in good times, but a customer looks to the bank for facilities when the pinch comes, and if, when the pinch comes, the bank itself is obliged to draw in its resources, to call in money, it disturbs the whole of the mercantile arrangements, and the bank is not really assisting the country, but is thwarting the best interests of the banking and trading communities. Listen to the figures. The *Economist* estimates the total deposits on current account held by all the banks in the United Kingdom, excluding the Bank of England, in July 1880, at from £470,000,000 to £480,000,000; and in July, 1890, at from £600,000,000 to £620,000,000, an increase in those ten years of £130,000,000. I cannot tell you, because I have not got the materials at my command, to what extent they increased their reserve in cash in proportion to the enormous increase in their liabilities; but I can give you some indication by the published accounts of some of the largest banks. According to the *Economist*, again, the liabilities of eleven large banks were, in 1879, £126,000,000, while their cash in hand, or at the Bank of England, amounted to £16,200,000 ; in 1889 the liabilities had risen to nearly £170,000,000, during those 11 years an increase of £44,000,000, but the cash balances had risen in the same time only to £17,500,000, an increase of £1,300,000. Observe the operation—£45,000,000 increase in liabilities to depositors; increase in cash reserve to meet them £1,300,000. I hope I shall not give offence, but I say I do not consider that a perfectly satisfactory position. On further examination I find the proportion of cash to liabilities had fallen during the 10 years from 12·9 to 10·3, a decrease of 2·6 on 12·9, which is about one-fifth of the whole reserve. During these ten years the change is that you have only four-fifths of the reserve, instead of five-fifths you had before; and in the case of one bank the percentage of cash to liabilities had sunk from nearly 22 per cent. to 12 per cent.; and in another case, where the percentages had fallen from 10 per cent. to a little over 6 per cent., the cash balance against the total liabilities of £9,000,000 was less than £600,000. A good deal of public attention has been called to these facts. It has been shown that while the liabilities to the public have enormously increased, the reserve has actually fallen. The reserve, let me make you clearly understand, is cash in the till or cash at the Bank of England. Some banks include cash on call, but cash on call is no reserve in the general sense so far as the community is concerned, because it means when you call in your money on call that you are embarrassing another person, while you may be relieving yourself. Let the public understand this—there is only a limited amount of money so unemployed. If everybody employs money up to the hilt there will be no unemployed money to come to the rescue in times of crisis. If you employ the money by lending it to another person you lend it to a broker. That broker cannot find the money except by going somewhere else. He goes somewhere else, and the whole in the end concentrates itself upon the Bank of England, and there is no reserve to a bank in having money on call in the sense in which I am now discussing reserves. Money on call is a valuable asset, but it is not an asset which constitutes a reserve useful to the general interests of the community at large.

" Now the banks, I believe, have taken up this position, viz.:—that it is no good to hold large reserves, and that they have simply to put their money into the hands of the Bank of England, with the result that the Bank of England would then make interest upon that money. But look at the late crisis. What was the establishment upon which the whole community relied when the time of crisis came ? It was the Bank of England, and the bankers themselves had to strengthen their reserves at the Bank of England, and were not able to bring that general alleviation to the community at large which was extended by the Bank of England. I am most anxious to avoid saying anything which may reflect upon our great banking institutions. They have done immense service to the country. They have brought together in their deposits capital which, being lent out again, has had fertilizing influences, and has assisted the commerce and the industry of this country. I say nothing against them. But I say it is a false system, and a dangerous system, to rely simply upon the aid the Bank of England can give in a crisis, and to take no thought whatever to meet the difficulties which might arise, except by such action as the Bank of England might possibly take, as they think, with the Government behind the Bank of England."

The figures quoted by Mr. Goschen understate the facts of the case. The same principle which he applies to " money at call " must be applied to " cash " reserves. He explains that " cash on call is no reserve in the general sense so far as the community is concerned, because it means when you call in your money on call that you are embarrassing another person, while you may be relieving yourself." Apply this to the " cash " reserves of the banks entrusted to the care of the Bank of England. Of the eleven large joint-stock banks referred to by Mr. Goschen, their cash in hand and at the Bank of England at the end of June, 1879, was £17,500,000. This amount may be divided into two parts—the money in their own vaults, the great bulk of which is till money, and cannot, therefore, be regarded as "reserve"; and the balances at the Bank of England, which that Institution employs in its ordinary business. And if the balance at the Bank of England is called in, " you are embarrassing another person (sic.' the

Bank of England), while you may be relieving yourself."

It is very important to clearly understand this, and, with a view to still further impress his audience as to the nature of cash at call, Mr. Goschen illustrated it further. "If everybody employs money up to the hilt, there will be no unemployed money to come to the rescue in time of crisis. If you employ the money by lending it to another person you lend it to a broker. That broker cannot find the money except by going somewhere else. He goes somewhere else, and the whole in the end concentrates itself upon the Bank of England, and there is no reserve to a bank in having money on call in the sense in which I am now discussing reserves. Money on call is a valuable asset, but it is not an asset which constitutes a reserve useful to the general interests of the community at large." Now the difference in the mode of a bank obtaining its money at call and its balance at the Bank, so far as it concentrates itself upon the Bank of England, is that in one case its action is direct, and in the other indirect. If the cash which—in Mr. Goschen's illustration—was placed at call with the broker had gone to swell the balance at the Bank, there would still

" be no unemployed money to come to the rescue
in time of panic ": if the bank wanted the money
the Bank of England would have to produce it.
So that whether a bank places its money at call,
or deposits it at the Bank, if it is required the
drain, in either case, concentrates itself upon the
Bank of England

Perhaps this will be more clearly realised if the
cash reserves of the banks which are not in the
Clearing House, and which keep their cash reserves at a Clearing House bank—other than
the Bank of England—are considered. Suppose
the Clearing House bank is the London and
Westminster. The balance at the London and
Westminster Bank is employed in the same way
as its other deposits ; and, therefore, that is "no
reserve in the general sense, so far as the community is concerned, because it means when you
call in your money on call (or your balance at
another bank) that you are embarrassing another
person (the London and Westminster Bank), while
you may be relieving yourself." What does the
London and Westminster Bank do? It draws
on its balance at the Bank of England, "and the
whole in the end concentrates itself upon the
Bank of England, and there is no reserve to a

bank in having money on call (or a balance at another bank) in the sense in which I am now discussing reserves."

In a similar way all the financial operations of the country concentrate themselves upon the Bank of England, and there is "no unemployed money to come to the rescue in time of panic," except the reserve in the Banking Department of the Bank of England. Of course if the panic is of only a limited character, and the money withdrawn from one bank is placed in another, no fresh money is required. But when the drain reduces the total amount of the deposits in all the banks, it concentrates itself entirely upon the only store of unused cash, viz.:—the reserve of the Banking Department of the Bank of England.

The *Economist*, commenting upon Mr. Goschen's speech on the 31st Jan., 1891, has, to some extent, pointed out the effect upon the figures he made use of by the practice of placing the reserves of one set of banks as balances at another. It says :—" Against liabilities amounting to many hundreds of millions, all of which are payable in gold, our joint-stock bank reserves are so small as to be utterly insignificant. Some figures which we recently gave to show upon how narrow a basis of actual cash the huge fabric of our banking credit rests, were quoted by Mr. Goschen, and may be worth repeating. At the end of June, 1879, the liabilities of eleven large London Joint-Stock Banks amounted to nearly £170,000,000, while their cash in hand and at the Bank of England did not exceed £17,500,000. Of this cash, however, only a portion can be regarded as constituting an available reserve. Probably about £9,000,000 of it is deposited with the Bank of England, and of that sum a certain proportion is required to meet Clearing-house debts, &c., and is thus of the nature not of a reserve, but of a working balance. So also with the cash which the banks retain in their own hands. The great bulk of that is simply till money. It is needed for ordinary day-to-day disbursements, and is not available to meet exceptional demands, which is what a reserve is needed for. And even the cash deposited with the Bank of England is not kept intact. It is used by the Bank in exactly the same way as its other deposits are used. From 40 to 50 per cent. of it is kept in reserve, while the remainder is employed in the ordinary way of business. Thus

of the £17,500,000 of cash shown in the balance-
sheets, it may be doubted whether as much as
£8,000,000 or £9,000,000 exists anywhere as an
immediately available cash reserve. The tendency of late years, moreover, has been to work
with smaller and smaller balances of free cash.
The proportion of cash to liabilities to the public,
which in the case of the banks we are dealing
with, was 12·9 per cent. in 1871, had shrunk in
1889 to 10·3 per cent.; and in the latter year,
the immediately available cash reserve of the
banks probably did not much, if at all, exceed
5 per cent. of their liabilities."

Thus, Mr. Goschen's proportion of cash reserve
to the deposits of the 11 banks referred to comes
down from 10·3 per cent. to 5 per cent. But
what is the result if the effect of the practice of
placing the reserves of one set of banks as
balances at another is still further examined ?
The 11 banks which were selected were Clearing-
house banks, who deposit their reserves directly
with the Bank of England; but where are the
cash reserves of the non-Clearing banks ? They
form part of the deposits of the Clearing-house
banks, and have been absorbed in their general
business, just in the same way as the balances

of the Clearing-house banks have been absorbed in the general business of the Bank of England.

In order, therefore, to ascertain the actual proportion of unused cash to the deposits of the banks, at the periods referred to by Mr. Goschen, we will take the total deposits of all the banks, including the Bank of England, and deduct from that amount say 10 per cent.— as representing the reserves of banks deposited with other banks, and so included in the total amount of deposits—and see what proportion the reserve of the Bank of England (the only available cash reserve in the country) bore to those totals in 1879, and in 1889 respectively.

In July, 1880, taking the medium figures given by Mr. Goschen, the total deposits held by all the banks in the United Kingdom, excluding the Bank of England, were £475,000,000; the Bank of England's deposits averaged for the year, 1879, £37,000,000, making a total of £512,000,000. From this deduct 10 per cent., which is a very liberal estimate of the reserves of banks deposited with other banks, and so included in the total amount of the deposits, leaving £461,000,000 due to the public. Against this, the only reserve of

unused cash in the country (with the exception of
the reserve in the Issue Department of the Bank
of England which is specially set apart to secure
the convertibility of the bank-notes,) was the
reserve of the Banking Department of the Bank
of England, which averaged for the year 1879,
£18,000,000.   So that the proportion of cash
reserve against the deposits of all the banks in
the United Kingdom, including the Bank of
England, was 3·9 per cent.   That is to say
a drain of 3·9 per cent. of the banks' deposits,
either as the result of panic, or for the purpose of
export, or partly on account of panic, and partly
on account of liabilities to foreign countries, would
have exhausted all the available cash in the
country.

In July, 1890, the total deposits held by all the
banks in the United Kingdom, excluding the
Bank of England, were £610,000,000; the Bank
of England's deposits averaged for the year
1889, £33,000,000 making a total of £643,000,000.
Deduct 10 per cent. for the reserves of banks
deposited with other banks, leaving a liability of
£579,000,000.   The reserve of the Bank of
England for the year 1889, averaged £13,000,000,
so that the proportion of cash reserve against

the total deposits of all the banks was 2·2 per cent.

Thus, a comparison of the proportion of cash to liabilities for the two periods under review shows a reduction from 3·9 per cent. to 2·2, a decrease of 1·7 on 3·9, which is over 43 per cent. of the whole reserve. What Mr. Goschen regarded as so unsatisfactory in the case he furnished of the 11 joint-stock banks was a falling off in the proportion of cash to liabilities "during the ten years from 12·9 to 10·3, a decrease of 2·6 on 12·9, which is about one-fifth of the whole reserve." But the actual proportion of available cash to the liabilities of all the banks is only 2·2 per cent., instead of 10·3; and the falling off in the ten years instead of being 20 per cent. of the whole reserve is over 43 per cent.

A falling off in ten years of over 43 per cent. in the cash reserve held against the liabilities of the banks, may be taken as an indication that they do not recognise any connection between the two. They do not. That they ought to do so everyone will admit; but the difficulty is how to bring this about. The system of reliance upon the Bank of England in times of exceptional difficulty has grown out of the ancient privileges no longer existing, and the *préstige* of that Institution. The Bank of England goes on managing its business with respect to its reserve in the same way that it always has done : the other banks conduct their business in the same way as they did when—as Mr. Goschen puts it—"the Bank of England was an Institution so vastly greater than all the others that it was able to command the money market and impose its terms".; but, as he adds, "those times have changed." Nevertheless, the practice of the banks has not changed, and the system remains by which any exceptional drain concentrates itself upon the Bank of England, whilst the Bank of England regulates its reserve in proportion to the total of its own liabilities, irrespective of the total liabilities of all the banks. In the two periods referred to above, the liabilities of the Bank of England in 1879, averaged 37 millions, and its reserve 18 millions; but in 1889 its liabilities were reduced to an average of 33 millions, and its reserve to 13 millions. The fact, that the liabilities of the other banks had, in the meantime, enormously increased, and that they had made no provision for a cash reserve against their increased liabilities, did not prevent the Bank allowing its reserve to be reduced simultaneously with a reduction of its own liabilities, although in a time of difficulty any drain resulting from the increased liabilities of the other banks would have concentrated itself upon the Bank of England. Mr. Weguelin said the principle on which the directors of the Bank of England regulated their reserve was to keep from one-fourth to one-third of the liabilities as a reserve; Mr. Hankey considered about a third as the proportion of reserve to liability at which the Bank should aim; since then the pressure of public opinion has resulted in a larger proportion, and the reserve is nearer 40 per cent. of the liabilities; but it is not in any way regulated by the total deposits of all the banks.

The other banks have not sufficient inducement to keep adequate cash reserves. It pays them better to invest in first-class securities; and the only limit to their doing so is the risk of loss which they incur by the difference in the buying and selling price of the securities, and the brokerage. It is, therefore, good policy on their part not to invest money which they are likely to require in the ordinary course of their business. But what motive is there to induce them to keep a portion of their funds idle in order to meet the emergency of a panic which happens about every ten years? In that event they can borrow on their Consols, say for three months, at 10 per cent. per annum (the rate fixed by the Government when the Bank Charter Act is suspended), whilst for the ten years they invest in Consols they earn $2\frac{1}{2}$ per cent. per annum. This means to a bank that might require a loan of £100,000 on its Consols, that it would have to pay £2,500 for interest for say three months of pressure; whereas in the previous ten years, at simple interest, it has earned £25,000.

Moreover, before the banks generally are likely to increase the amount of money they may have idle, they will naturally consider what has become of the amount they have hitherto kept unemployed. What is the reply? If a country bank has kept a large balance with its London agent it has become absorbed in the general business of the London bank, and only a small proportion of it has found its way to the London banker's balance at the Bank of England. Similarly the amount which the London bank has kept with the Bank of England has been absorbed in the business of that Institution, and only a proportion has been kept in reserve. If, therefore, the banks generally thought it expedient to add to the reserve at the Bank of England they would find, according to the present system, that whatever sums they appropriated for that purpose would have to go through one or two filters before it reached its destination.

This system, however, is approved of by the present Governor of the Bank of England. He said at the half-yearly meeting of the Bank on the 12th March last :—" The principle of the existing system of finance in this country is a very good one. The only question that has been raised is, whether under competition and in the pursuit of economy, it has not been pushed a little further than is consistent with the interests of trade and commerce. Where reserves are small, any "pull" upon them by withdrawals for foreign countries necessarily makes a large reduction in our reserve ; and, as I have already explained, as that reserve is practically the reserve of the country—the only (other) money being the till money of the Bank (? banks), the reduction has a much larger effect upon the value of money than it would have if the balances were larger. It is only in that respect that I consider the existing system has failed in the past."

This language is in striking contrast to Mr. Goschen's. The Governor admits that the reserve of the Bank of England is " practically the reserve of the country " ; and he knows that the claim has been made through the late Mr. R. C. L. Bevan, on behalf of the joint-stock banks, and more recently by Mr. Bagehot in " Lombard Street," that it should keep a reserve in order that it may grant accommodation to whoever should require it. But he apparently sees no objection to this. The only defect in the system which he perceives is, that in consequence of the small amount of surplus cash the money market is very sensitive, and the interests of trade and commerce suffer because the value of money fluctuates more than it would do if a larger amount was kept. Well, perhaps this is not so strange if the report is correct that on the occasion of the recent " Baring crisis," the directors of the Bank were able to obtain the consent of the Government to the suspension of the Bank Charter Act before the firm's difficulties became known to the public. Of course, if the Bank of England are allowed to issue an unlimited number of demands upon the property of the note-holders whenever an emergency arises, it matters very little to the Bank what claims are made upon it. The Chancellor of the Exchequer is, however, in a very different position. He finds that the onus of the insufficiency of the cash reserves of the banks devolves upon him, and in an extremity he is called upon to authorise a violation of the law. His opinion of the present system, therefore, materially differs from that of the Governor of the Bank. He expresses himself as follows :—" I say it is a false system and a dangerous system to rely simply upon the aid the Bank of England can give in a crisis, and to take no thought whatever to meet the difficulties which might arise, except by such action as the Bank of England may possibly take as they think, with the Government behind the Bank of England."

For this reason it devolves upon the Government to find means by which they will protect themselves as far as possible from being "squeezed," as a last resource, in the future. Mr. Goschen referred to the position of the Government in the matter as follows:—" In the most friendly spirit I would indicate to the banks of this country that the public have an enormous interest in the proportion of the reserve which they hold to deposits. They all hold together; and you have this remarkable fact, that the soundest and strongest banks may be making the smallest dividends, whilst the more imprudent banks, who invest the depositors' money, leaving a small reserve, are able to show much larger dividends to their shareholders. Why are the latter able to take this course? Because they have the conviction that the failure of any one of these big banks would be such a disaster to the whole community that the other banks would be compelled to come to their assistance, and to rescue the offending bank from the consequence of its offences by themselves undertaking a part of their liabilities. The more imprudent banks will say, 'There is no imprudence. We shall never be allowed to fail; our fellow bankers must come to our assistance, and, if not our fellow bankers, then the Bank of England; and if not the Bank of England, then the Government.' I say that gives us a *locus standi*, and in the same way as the Government has had a *locus standi* with regard to shipping, and has said that excessive cargoes shall not be carried because they are dangerous to the safety of the public, the question may arise whether the public might have the right to say that no excessive cargo shall be carried by banks receiving public money—that business shall be conducted in a manner which shall be considered safe by the community at large."

In this chapter we have presented the difficulties of the problem; in the next we shall see what use Mr. Goschen proposes to make of his *locus standi* in the matter.

CHAPTER V.

THE PUBLICATION OF ACCOUNTS.

IN the course of Mr. Goschen's speech he suggested four methods of dealing with the deficiency of the banks' reserves, and in the following order. In the first place he referred to America, where the State compels the banks to retain 25 per cent. in reserve against their deposits, and declared that he would "never propose to impose such an iron system upon the great banking institutions of this country." In the second place he said there were suggestions that "if there was an excess of deposits and liabilities, up beyond a certain line, then that should be done which is done in some foreign lands, they should have to pay a certain tax upon the excess of their deposits"; and with regard to this he said, "I will not say what view I hold upon such a suggestion." Thirdly, he said "there is one measure which I think may fairly be taken, and which the public would have a right to demand, and that is, the more frequent publication of accounts." And fourthly, he said if there was an effort made in the direction of co-operation as to the publication of accounts, he could see that "measures might be taken to establish what I have indicated as a second reserve for the country at large," realised by the issue of £1 notes.

The two suggestions which are within measurable distance of being acted upon are the two last. The first of these, the one proposing a more frequent publication of the accounts of the joint-stock banks, has already been taken into consideration by the London joint-stock banks, and they have decided to publish monthly accounts. The result which is anticipated by Mr. Goschen is thus explained:—"The public have the advantage of the publication of the Banks' return. It is a barometer—an important barometer to all you men of business. But a barometer is fallacious. At the same time, you are able to check and control the results which you will draw from those barometrical readings, by your studying the position of these great institutions, as mighty in their way as the Bank of England, holding great deposits, the condition of which is of such vast importance to every trader, to every manufacturer, to every commercial centre in this country."

The Governor of the Bank of England, at

the last meeting of its proprietors, has also given an exposition of the view of the Chancellor of the Exchequer in requiring a more frequent publication of accounts. He stated that the Chancellor of the Exchequer had said "he has held that the publication of accounts—he has not had time to fix any period, whether weekly or fortnightly—but that the publication of accounts more frequently than half-yearly would be an advantage, because where banks were behind the line, and kept poorer reserves than they ought to do, the effect of public opinion on those banks would be to bring them up to the standard of others." The more frequent publication of the accounts of the joint-stock banks may possibly be the means of increasing their cash balances; but to what extent is it likely to meet the difficulties referred to in the previous chapter? If the country banks increase their balances they will add to the liabilities of their London agents, who will perhaps on that account increase their balance with the Bank of England in proportion to the amount which that increase bears to their total deposits. To take an example: On the 31st December last the liabilities of the London and Westminster Bank on current and deposit ac-

counts were £25,800,000, and its cash in hand at
the Bank of England was £3,984,000. Now,
suppose one of the country banks depositing with
it had been in the habit of keeping a balance of
£500,000 more than was its actual practice. That
money would have been employed in the ordinary
business of the London and Westminster Bank.
The result would be—taking a similar proportion
of cash to liabilities as now exists—that its
liabilities would be £26,300,000, and the reserve
£4,061,000. That is to say that the effect of a
country bank adding an extra £500,000 to its
balance, would only add to the "reserve in the
general sense so far as the community is concerned" to the extent of £77,000.

The result would be different in degree if the
London clearing-house joint-stock banks added to
their balances at the Bank of England, because
they would not be filtered on the way. In their
case 40 per cent. of the increased balance would
be added to the "reserve in the general sense so
far as the country is concerned," as the Bank of
England keeps that proportion of its deposits in
cash.

The more frequent publication of accounts is
not, therefore, calculated to induce bankers

voluntarily to add to the amount of their balances with a view to increasing the ultimate reserve of available cash, so long as only a fraction of the amount they keep idle finds its way to the reserve.

But it is imagined that if the accounts are published more frequently, public opinion will be brought to bear upon those banks who keep small cash balances. The Chancellor of the Exchequer is said to have expressed his opinion that "where banks were behind the line, and kept poorer reserves than they ought to do, the effect of public opinion on those banks would be to bring them up to the standard of others."

Take the last accounts published by the London and Westminster Bank and the Union Bank of London. The liabilities of the London and Westminster, excepting to shareholders, were £26,958,000, and the cash in hand and at the Bank of England was £3,984,000, showing a percentage of 14·7; the liabilities of the Union Bank were £16,809,000, and the cash in hand and at the Bank of England was £2,814,000, showing a percentage of 16·7. So that the cash reserve to liabilities of the Union Bank is 2 per cent. on 14·7; that is 13·6 per cent. more than that of

the London and Westminster Bank. Will the effect
of public opinion on the London and Westminster
Bank bring its reserve up to the standard of the
Union Bank? Before the public formed an
opinion as to which bank kept the larger proportion of its assets in an available form, they would
want to know something more than the actual
amount of cash in hand. They would enquire
into the amount of money at call, and first-class
investments, held by each. And what would be
the result? They would find the proportion of
cash, money at call and short notice, and investments to liabilities, held by the London and
Westminster was 57 per cent.; and by the Union
only 49 per cent. Would public opinion under
such circumstances be brought to bear on the
London and Westminster to increase its cash reserve? Of the two banks the public would probably prefer the position of the one which had a
larger proportion of cash and readily convertible
securities to liabilities. They would say if the
London and Westminster Bank wants more cash
it can any morning sell its Consols, and other
first-class securities, and its cash would then bear
a larger proportion to its liabilities than the Union
Bank would hold if it also sold its securities. But

the probability is that the general public would
care for none of these things. The distinction
between cash and securities readily convertible
into cash is too refined for the ordinary public.
And if the shareholders of either Bank thought
about the matter at all, the shareholders of the
Union Bank might point out that they might be
making larger profits if they followed the example
of the London and Westminster Bank and invested a similar proportion of their funds.

There is, moreover, another aspect of the
question which must be taken into consideration
before any useful opinion can be formed as to the
relative proportions of cash reserves to deposits.
Deposits may be divided into two classes: those
repayable on demand, and those repayable after
notice. The proportion of cash which should be
kept in reserve to meet these essentially distinct
forms of liability is on quite a different scale.
Where time has to elapse before the demand
becomes effective an opportunity is afforded to a
bank to realise its assets if necessary. A notice
of withdrawal is given, and the bank can either
realise its securities, or reduce the amount of its
advances. And the money required under notice
of withdrawal given in a panic, will probably not

be required by the time the term of the notice for
re-payment expires. Panics are generally very
virulent while they last; but they do not last
long. The amount of cash necessary to be
reserved in order to cover a liability for the re-
payment of money due on demand is, obviously,
very much larger than is required to cover a
liability for money not due until the expiration
of notice. So that the publication by a bank of
the amount due on demand, and after notice, in
one total, gives no indication of the proportion of
cash to liabilities which should be reserved. Who
can tell what portion of the London and Westminster's liabilities of £26,958,000 are due on
demand, and what portion do not become payable
until after notice. It is quite possible that a more
definite knowledge of the amounts which go to
make up the total liabilities of the London and
Westminster and the Union Banks respectively,
would make it clear that the assumption that the
Union Bank's cash reserve is larger in proportion
to liabilities than that of the London and Westminster is altogether illusory. If the proportion
of liabilities due by the Union Bank on demand
to those due after notice is substantially greater
than that of the London and Westminster, the

apparently larger cash reserve is a delusion. And without further information, it is quite hopeless for the public to endeavour to form any opinion as to the relative cash reserves of the two banks; and, consequently, to bring to bear any influence in bringing up the reserve of the one to the standard of the other.

Upon this point " Lombard Street" speaks clearly and forcibly (p. 301):—" That the amount of the liabilities of a bank is a principal element in determining the proper amount of its reserve is plainly true; but that it is the only element by which that amount is determined is plainly false. The intrinsic nature of these liabilities must be considered, as well as their numerical quantity. For example, no one would say that the same amount of reserve ought to be kept against acceptances which cannot be paid except at a certain day, and against deposits at call, which may be demanded at any moment. If a bank groups these liabilities together in the balance-sheet, you cannot tell the amount of reserve it ought to keep. The necessary information is not given you.

" Nor can you certainly determine the amount of reserve necessary to be kept against deposits

unless you know something as to the nature
of these deposits. If out of £3,000,000 of
money, one depositor has £1,000,000 to his
credit, and may draw it out when he pleases, a
much larger reserve will be necessary against
that liability of £1,000,000 than against the
remaining £2,000,000. The *intensity* of the
liability, so to say, is much greater; and therefore the provision in store must be much greater
also. On the other hand, supposing that this
single depositor is one of calculable habits—
suppose that it is a public body, the time of
whose demands is known, and the time of whose
receipts is known also—this single liability requires a less reserve than that of an equal amount
of ordinary liabilities. The danger that it will
be called for is much less; and therefore the
security taken against it may be much less too.
Unless the quality of the liabilities is considered
as well as their quantity, the due provision for
their payment cannot be determined."

From this it will be seen that supposing all the
banks published similar forms of account, showing
what portion of their liabilities were payable (1)
on demand, (2) after notice and (3) at fixed
dates—such as acceptances—it would even then

be difficult for the public to come to the conclusion that the 14·7 per cent. reserve of the London and Westminster was not equivalent to the 16·7 per cent. of the Union Bank. At the same time if the liabilities were divided in this way, it would afford a very much better indication of the position of affairs than can possibly be arrived at from balance sheets which make no distinction between liabilities payable on demand and those payable at some future date. And until an alteration takes place in the form of the accounts their publication will be useless for the purpose of barometrical readings.

Similarly with regard to the return of the Bank of England. That barometer might be greatly improved. On the one hand the total deposits might be divided into (1) Government balances, (2) bankers' balances, and (3) other balances. And on the other hand it might show the amount of the (1) bills discounted, (2) advances on security, and (3) the investments of the Bank. If this barometer was thus amended a much better judgment upon the probable course of events could be formed. From time to time efforts have been made in this direction; but as a matter of fact the Bank now gives less information about its

transactions than it did formerly. Particulars of
the amounts of bills discounted, and of the tem-
porary advances used to be regularly published in
returns furnished to the Government, but these
figures have not been continued since 1875.
Speaking of this on the 19th June, 1879, at a
meeting of the Institute of Bankers Mr. J. Herbert
Tritton (Messrs. Barclay and Co.) said :—" If the
directors of the Bank of England would resume
the publication of the amount of discounts which
they hold, it would be of material service to us in
considering many questions which are now crop-
ping up in connection with the currency of the
country. Then there is another item. The Bank
of England has been referred to, very properly,
as the " Bankers' Bank." That is its pre-eminent
position in this country ; and that being so, many
of us would gladly hail the publication of the
bankers' balances in a separate form as distinguished from the other deposits. It has been,
as you are aware, published from time to time
under the pressure of a Parliamentary return; but
when that pressure was withdrawn the publication
was also withdrawn."

The more frequent and more full publication of
accounts by the Bank of England and the other

banks would enable the public to form a much
better opinion of the probable course of the money
market than they can do with only the weekly
return of the Bank of England to guide them.
The money market has outgrown its dependence
upon that Institution. When the Bank of England was all-powerful in the market the information which its returns furnished was a sufficient
indication of the probable value of money in the
immediate future. But as the Bank has gradually
lost its control of the market it has become
important to observe the operations of the other
banks; and any additional means of " studying
the position of the great joint stock banks, as
mighty in their way as the Bank of England " is
to be welcomed. It would be too sanguine to
expect all the banks to publish their accounts in
the full manner suggested above. But there
seems no reason why the Bank of England should
not give the total amount of the bankers' balances
every week. Then the public would know what
was the amount of unemployed money in the
market. At present only the amount of the Bank
of England's unemployed money is made known.
If the amount of the bankers' balances was also
published it would be seen whether when the Bank

raised its rate of discount the other banks would be likely to follow suit. If the bankers' balances were abnormally large some time would generally take place before the Bank of England could produce a sufficient effect upon the market to turn the foreign exchanges in our favour as the other bankers wishing to reduce their surplus would discount below the Bank of England rate. On the other hand when the bankers' balances are below the average amount and the Bank rate is raised it at once becomes the market rate.

It is difficult to exaggerate the importance of any information which would enable the mercantile community to better understand the influence which the raising of the bank rate is likely to exercise in attracting specie. In years gone by this was a most effective instrument in settling the value of money. The other banks followed the lead of the Bank of England. But it no longer commands the same proportionate amount of the markets' available capital as it did formerly. The rate of discount which affects the exchanges is not that which is published by the Bank of England, but the market rate, which is determined by the supply and demand of the whole of the floating capital in the market. The

Bank of England is only one of the many institutions whose floating capital goes to make the rate of discount which determines the state of the exchanges; and as the businesses of the other banks and the discount houses increase, and the business of the Bank of England remains practically stationary, the Bank of England's power in the market is a constantly diminishing quantity, and it is less and less able to affect the value of money even temporarily. The growing impotence of the Bank of England to regulate the value of money by the Bank rate was illustrated in a very striking manner in 1877. On October 4th, the reserve having been reduced from £11,895,257 to £9,721,123 the Bank raised its rate from 3 to 4 per cent., but the market rate was only $2\frac{3}{4}$ per cent; on October 11th the rate was raised to 5 per cent., but the market rate did not follow, and on the 5th November, with the reserve only £9,678,797, the Bank rate 5 per cent.; and the market rate of discount only $3\frac{1}{4}$ per cent.; the London and Westminster Bank (whose lead was followed by the other joint stock banks on the 9th November) determined no longer to follow the Bank rate in fixing the rate of interest it allows on its deposits. The Bank of

England had done all it could to replenish its reserves : it was doing little or no discount business.
But as the other banks had a large amount of
unemployed money—their balances with the Bank
of England amounting to £10,069,000 (more than
the Bank of England's reserve), they competed
with each other to such an extent as to render
the official rate of the Bank ineffective as a means
to protect its reserve. The Bank of England rate
might just as well have stood at $3\frac{1}{2}$ per cent. as at 5
per cent. so far as its influence in attracting gold
from abroad was concerned. Anyone who wanted
gold for export had merely to go to his bankers
or billbrokers, get his bills discounted at the
market rate of $3\frac{1}{4}$ per cent.; place the proceeds
with his bankers ; obtain bank notes ; and then
take them to the Bank to be exchanged for gold.

The publication of the amount of the "bankers'
balances" from week to week would put the
public on their guard against the most dangerous
point in our single reserve system. If our system
of finance was a natural one, instead of having
grown out of the monopoly of "exclusive banking" enjoyed by the Bank of England in former
years, every bank would keep its reserve of unemployed money in its own custody instead of

banking it with the Bank of England. In that case if it had a larger surplus than it deemed sufficient for its requirements, the increased money it would place on the market would come from its own store of unused cash. Whereas, by our one-reserve system, the money which it withdraws from its balance has to be provided out of the Bank of England's reserve. It is, therefore, of supreme moment that the amount of the bankers' balances should be watched with most jealous care. For the Bank of England, in times of plentiful and cheap money to allow its reserve to be depleted simultaneously with an increase in the amount of the "bankers' balances" is to court future trouble. It is more important to know what proportion the Bank's reserve bears to the " bankers' balances " from time to time, than to know what proportion it bears—as we now rely upon exclusively—to the total liabilities.

The amount of the " bankers' balances " is the principal guide to the amount of money seeking employment; and before the Bank of England's rate of discount can act upon the Exchanges, the Bank has in some way to reduce the amount of floating capital to its ordinary proportions. Hence it is that the Bank sometimes becomes a large borrower, or seller, in the market. The extent of its operations in this direction is chiefly regulated by the amount of the "bankers' balances," and the longer it takes to effect its object the more acute and sensitive does the market become. A healthy public opinion that the Bank's reserve ought, as a rule, to grow with the amount of the "banker's balances," instead of as now being only brought to bear on the proportion of reserve to total liabilities, would do much to steady the market, and to remedy what the Governor of the Bank has described as the failure of the existing system of finance in the past, viz., the much larger effect upon the value of money resulting from any "pull" upon the reserve, by with-drawals for foreign countries where reserves are small.

The weekly publication of the amount of the "bankers' balances," and the other alterations which have been suggested with a view to the improvement of the barometers afforded by the accounts of the Bank of England and the other banks, would be of immense advantage to the mercantile community. But it is altogether a mistake to suppose that the more frequent publication of accounts, which do not even distinguish the deposits payable on demand from those payable after notice, can possibly contribute to the formation of a useful public opinion as to the amount of money which should be kept unemployed by the respective banks. And, moreover, there is the fundamental difficulty as to what is " overtrading," or " trading up to the hilt." It will generally be defined as an undue locking-up of resources : the employment in banking advances of an excessive amount of a bank's deposits. The investment of a bank's surplus over and above the amount employed in its business in first-class securities would not be regarded in the City as " overtrading." Money so invested is considered quite as available as money deposited with the Bank of England or some other bank. It would be considered a misnomer to call the investment of a surplus a " trading up to the hilt." And no bank that invested a large portion of its surplus in this way would suffer in comparison with a bank which allowed its surplus to remain idle. Depositers are quite as satisfied with the safety of their money in a bank which has its surplus largely invested in first-class securities, as in a bank which keeps a greater proportion of its surplus with another bank.

To trust, therefore, to the more frequent publication of accounts which do not supply the necessary data upon which it is possible to estimate what would be a proper amount of cash reserve to deposits; to the effect of a public opinion which does not regard it as any detriment to a bank to have a small cash reserve provided it has a large amount of investment in first-class securities; to bring to bear an influence upon those banks whose cash reserves are behind the line, is fatuous.

CHAPTER VI.

ONE POUND NOTES.

THE other proposal which is likely to assume a practical form relates to the issue of £1 notes. Mr. Goschen did not propound his plan with much clearness, and in concluding his speech he said :— " I feel, and I painfully feel, and I ask your indulgence, and the indulgence of the public, and of my critics in this respect, that it is impossible within the limits, even the extreme limits, which your patience has allowed me to occupy to-night, to do justice to the large currency plan, or even to such modified suggestions as I have made. They cannot be understood simply from the utterances to which I have given expression to-night." After this warning one feels some hesitation in criticising what appears to be the scheme which Mr. Goschen's speech foreshadows. The speech, however, is public property, and was, no doubt, made with the object of promoting a discussion upon the topics introduced into it. If we mistake its meaning, in some respects, it will not be from any want of endeavour to grasp it.

The object, and the object alone, for which Mr. Goschen is prepared to embark in any scheme such as the £1 note, is to increase the stock of gold at the centre in order to be stronger both for banking and for national purposes. He did not elaborate his plan to effect this object, but he declares that for the administration of this new currency the machinery established by the Bank Charter Act would be useless, because he is " totally opposed to any measure which would simply end in the exportation of gold from the circulation of this country." This is a very extraordinary reason to give for not issuing the £1 notes under the Bank Charter Act, because by its provisions, for every £1 note that is issued, a corresponding amount of bullion must be deposited. There is nothing to prevent the Issue Department of the Bank of England now issuing £1 notes (for the Act says nothing at all as to the denomination of the notes to be issued), and retaining every sovereign which the notes replaced in its possession. But Mr. Goschen said:— " Now, there is a favourite measure in the air, which is the increase of the fiduciary issue; and

I

many persons think that would be an advantage.
An increase of the fiduciary issue means, as I
understand it, the substitution of paper for gold.
Now, supposing you were to issue £20,000,000 of
£1 notes, and they were to take the place of
£20,000,000 in sovereigns in the pockets of the
people, or the tills of the banks, what would
happen to this £20,000,000 of gold? It is the
opinion of those who are in favour of this substitution that £20,000,000 would be added to our
stock of gold. (A voice—'Yes.') No, that would
not be added to our stock of gold. It would go
to the reserve of the Bank of England for the
moment, but afterwards it would, like all our
gold be open to the world at large ; and the gold
which we had called in, replacing it by notes,
being added to the reserve at the Bank, would in
the first instance, as do all other additions to the
reserve, lower the rate of interest, would create
great speculation for the moment, and would lead
to the export of gold to other countries; and,
having substituted paper for gold, you would
find that really you had not strengthened the
reserve of gold except by a small portion, whatever it might be, that we might gain. I cannot
tell you the importance I attach to a thorough

understanding of the principle by the people at large. They believe that if we were to substitute paper for gold we could keep gold under the ordinary arrangements of our Bank Charter Act. It is nothing of the kind. Paper expels gold unless you take particular precautions to retain the gold; and for my part I am totally opposed to any measure which would simply end in the expulsion of gold from the circulation of this country."

There is a confusion of thought in this argument arising from a want of recognition of the fact that the Bank of England is divided into two departments—the Issue Department and the Banking Department. The £20,000,000 of gold referred to by Mr. Goschen, if issued under the ordinary arrangements of the Bank Charter Act, would undoubtedly go to the Issue Department of the Bank of England, because the notes could not be issued until the gold was deposited there; and the Issue Department could not part with that gold until the notes were presented to it for payment. Mr. Goschen's argument, on the other hand, is based upon the assumption that the gold would go to the reserve of the Banking Department of the Bank of England,

and be employed by it in its ordinary banking business. His theory that "paper expels gold unless you take particular precautions to retain the gold" is perfectly sound; but the precautions taken to retain the gold by the Bank Charter Act are of the most absolute character, and they are quite sufficient to attain the object, the object alone, for which Mr. Goschen is prepared to embark in any scheme such as the £1 note, viz., to increase the stock of gold at the centre.

It may be, however, that when Mr. Goschen was referring to the "ordinary arrangements of the Bank Charter Act," he did not intend to refer to them as they exist at present, but he was explaining what would be the effect of an issue of £1 notes provided the Act was so far modified as to increase the fiduciary basis of the issue to such an amount as would maintain a similar proportion of bullion to securities as there is at present. If that was his intention his illustration would have better defined his meaning if he had taken say £30,000,000 as his basis, and said that if that amount of £1 notes were issued upon a similar proportion of cash to securities which is now reserved in the Issue Department of the Bank of

England, say two-thirds—£20,000,000 would be retained in gold, and the remaining £10,000,000 issued upon securities, would be the means of expelling that amount of gold from the country.

Or, possibly, he was explaining what would be the effect if the Government authorised the Issue Department of the Bank of England, to issue £1 notes entirely upon securities instead of upon gold; which would seem to be borne out by his reference to the issue of £1 notes as " a favorite measure in the air, which is the increase of the fiduciary issue," and by the illustration which he used. But in that case the ordinary arrangements of the Bank Charter Act would have to be discontinued, and a new Act would have to be introduced to authorise an increase of notes upon securities. This would have the effect of reducing the proportion of bullion to securities, and would thereby considerably weaken the security given for the convertibility on demand of the existing notes. The present proportion of notes issued upon gold coin and bullion to those issued upon securities is about 130 per cent., but if £30,000,000 of £1 notes are to be issued upon securities only, the proportion will be reduced to about 45 per cent. A change of so startling a character that it seems extremely unlikely that Mr. Goschen would entertain it.

But, whatever may be the conditions upon which Mr. Goschen proposes to issue £1 notes—whether a similar proportion shall be issued upon gold to those issued upon securities, as in the case of the existing notes; or a different proportion; or wholly upon securities; the gold to be liberated by this means is to be retained, and to form the basis of a second reserve. A second reserve of gold upon the strength of which a further issue of notes may take place when the position of the country may seem to demand it. Mr. Goschen explains his proposal as follows:—"Any movement to which I would be a party in the direction of the fiduciary issue must have this result—that you must stop the gold; that the bullion and the gold which would be brought by the public in exchange for the £1 notes, or any other form of notes, should be dealt with in such a manner as not to leave the country. I would establish it as a second reserve, not to be put into the ordinary issue; but I would have a separate stock of gold realized to this country by a certain issue of paper money which was to be issued only when emergencies should

arise . . . . . . When, now, there is a
suspension of the Bank Charter Act, you suspend
the Bank Charter Act by a simple issue of paper,
unsupported by gold, and sometimes almost
adding to the dangers of the situation by increasing your paper money at a time when gold is
leaving the country. Well, it would be infinitely
better if there existed in this country a reserve
of gold, a separate stock of gold, with which
in time of emergency, the Bank of England would
be able to come to the rescue of the mercantile
community generally. My object would be to
establish a second reserve—a reserve which we
should be able to establish by means of a certain
fiduciary issue—and that this second reserve,
under conditions to be defined, should take the
place of the suspension of the Bank Charter Act
by providing the means of the further issue, by
safe notes, when the position of the country might
seem to demand it."

Any proposal to create a second reserve, and
thereby to avoid the necessity of suspensions of
the Bank Charter Act is entitled to favourable
consideration. And if, in order to effect so
desirable an object it is found necessary to somewhat lessen the proportion of notes issued upon

gold, to those issued upon securities, the advantages to be derived from doing so may outweigh that disadvantage, provided the process is not carried too far. But while fully sympathising with the object which Mr. Goschen has in view, there seems a fatal objection to the course he suggests. It is the proposal to place the Banking Department of the Bank of England in a position to command a supply of ready money in time of emergency so that it can " come to the rescue of the mercantile community generally." This proposal seems expressly designed to relieve all other banks from the responsibility of keeping adequate cash reserves of their own : it is for the Government to deliberately entrust the solvency of the whole mercantile community to the discretion of the directors of one Bank : it is to go back to the policy which led to so many disasters when the Bank of England had the exclusive power of manufacturing ready money before the Bank Charter Act, 1844, was passed : it is to perpetuate the evils resulting from other banks trusting to the Bank of England instead of to their own reserves.

This reliance upon the Bank of England in times of difficulty was unfortunately, to some extent, encouraged by Mr. Goschen. He condemned an absolute reliance upon the aid which the Bank might render, but he seemed to imply that there were some grounds for looking to the Bank for help of an exceptional character. For instance, he said: " I say it is a false system and a dangerous system to rely simply upon the aid the Bank of England can give in a crisis, and to take no thought whatever to meet the difficulties which might arise, except by such action as the Bank of England may possibly take, as they think, with the Government behind the Bank of England." The introduction of the word "simply" spoils the effect of this utterance. Why should other banks rely at all upon the aid the Bank of England can give in a crisis? Again, later on in his speech, Mr. Goschen said the Bank of England " has still the duty of endeavouring to meet all the necessities of a crisis; it still fills such a position that the whole of the country looks to it to extricate it from a difficulty, but it does not command any longer the same proportionate resources which it commanded in the old times. It is unable at this moment, in the face of this £600,000,000 of deposits entrusted to other banks, to take the same position as in times past."

This does not, perhaps, necessarily imply that there is any peculiar duty belonging to the Bank of England which does not pertain to any other bank, except the duty of the recognised premier bank of the country to set an example in dealing with a panic. Nevertheless, having regard to the claims which have been made upon the Bank of England, it would have been more satisfactory if Mr. Goschen had clearly defined the Bank's position in the matter. It would have been more satisfactory if he had pointed out that the other banks had no right to allow themselves to get into a position of difficulty, and expect the Bank of England to extricate them from it, since the Bank does not command any longer the power to manufacture legal tender as it did in the old times. Possibly if his language had been more precise on this point the "Daily News" (3rd Feb.) would not have been taking it quite as a matter of course within a week after his speech, that "It is the function of the Bank to throw oil on the water, and to provide a harbour of refuge when the storm takes place. It is so because the Bank is practically the Agent of the Government, and as the Government at present keeps what Mr. Goschen would call a second reserve in the shape of gold locked up to secure the convertibility of the bank note, the Bank has the onerous duty. Outside banks know it, and have acted upon it, and have made large profits."

Well, if outside banks have been relying upon the Bank to provide a harbour of refuge when the storm takes place, and have thereby made large profits, because of the reserve of gold locked up to secure the convertibility of the bank note, what may they be expected to do when a special reserve is created expressly for the purpose of enabling the Bank of England in time of emergency to " come to the rescue of the mercantile community generally " ? Mr. Goschen foresaw this danger and said :—" We shall only aggravate, we shall not alleviate, the position if any relief given in the hope of a second reserve, besides the first reserve, should have the effect of inducing the joint-stock banks to trade further up to the hilt than they have hitherto ; if we should encourage the belief that there is safety at the centre, and that therefore to any extent we may invest our deposits, and that we may rely, instead of holding our own reserves, on the action of the Bank of England and the Government." How does Mr. Goschen hope to avoid what appear to be the natural consequences of the establishment of a second reserve?

He relies (1) upon the effects likely to follow a more frequent publication of accounts; and (2) he says:—"Such a solution (as the establishment of a second reserve by means of an issue of £1 notes) would only be proper, such a solution could only be defended, if conditions were imposed which did not aggravate the situation at the time. It would be improper to touch such a store of gold if the exchanges were against this country. It would be improper to touch such a reserve if the rate of interest were not at such a point as to be likely to attract gold from other countries."

Let us contrast these two safeguards with those which will be removed when the proposed second reserve is established. With regard to the effects likely to follow a more frequent publication of accounts, they have been discussed in the previous chapter. Take the most sanguine view possible, and contrast that with the abolition of the necessity, in future, of the intervention of the Government to suspend the Bank Charter Act. The second reserve to be established by means of an issue of £1 notes is to "take the

place of the suspension of the Bank Charter Act
by providing the means of the further issue,
by safe notes, when the position of the country
might seem to demand it." Hitherto the fact
that it has been necessary to get the consent of
the Government before the reserve in the Issue
Department of the Bank of England could be
utilised has operated, to some extent, as a check
upon entire dependence upon the Bank in time
of difficulty. It has been taken as a matter of
course that in a time of crisis the Act would be
suspended, but there has always been some uncertainty as to the precise time when the intervention of the Government would take place, and,
consequently, there has been the risk to those
who most neglected their cash reserves, and the
readily convertible character of their assets, of
being unable to bear the strain until the relief
afforded by the suspension of the Act was granted.
But this uncertainty will no longer exist if the
directors of the Bank are to be invested with
power to issue notes whenever emergencies arise
without its being necessary for them to first
obtain the authority of the Executive Government. To do away, therefore, with the necessity
of obtaining the consent of the Government

before special relief can be afforded, is to remove a direct incentive to the self-interest of banks to keep reserves; and in substitution of this powerful motive, Mr. Goschen proposes to rely upon the influence of a public opinion to be formed by means of the more frequent publication of accounts, which do not supply the necessary *data* for the purpose.

Then with regard to the reservation that " it would be improper to touch such a store of gold if the exchanges were against this country. It would be improper to touch such a reserve if the rate of interest were not at such a point as to be likely to attract gold from other countries." Contrast this with the condition which the Government has always made as to the rate of interest to be charged when the Bank Charter Act has been suspended. The rate of interest sufficient to attract gold may be 4 per cent. It often does, and sometimes even less is sufficient. Whereas 10 per cent. was the minimum charge when the Bank Charter Act was suspended, and only on first class security, and for a very short term, could money be obtained at that. Whenever the Government consented to place the gold in the Issue Department of the Bank of England at the service of the market they took care that it should pay heavily for its use. Those were times of suffering and loss; but the second reserve is to be easily got-at-able. There is to be no anxiety as to when the Government will consider the pressure of the market sufficiently intense to authorise the Bank to make use of the second reserve ; and there is to be no minimum charge of 10 per cent. for the money when the second reserve is resorted to.

Under these circumstances is it not reasonable to conclude that if Mr. Goschen's proposals are carried out, the fears which he expressed will be realised, and we "shall only aggravate, we shall not alleviate, the position if any relief given in the hope of a second reserve, besides the first reserve, should have the effect of inducing the joint stock banks to trade further up to the hilt than they have hitherto; if we should encourage the belief that there is safety at the centre, and that therefore to any extent we may invest our deposits, and that we may rely, instead of holding our own reserves, on the action of the Bank of England and the Government."

Probably one of the first results to follow the establishment of a second reserve upon the conditions proposed would be a gradual diminution of the reserve of the Banking Department of the Bank of England.   As Mr. Goschen has put it:— " The position in former times was this, that the Bank of England was an Institution so vastly greater than all the others that it was able to command the money market and impose its terms. Those times are changed."   And in its present position it cannot protect its reserve. Time after time it has tried ineffectually to protect itself from a foreign drain ; and it has only succeeded in doing so when the City has become uneasy, and other lenders of money have held their hands because they feared a state of things might arise which would bring about a panic, and, consequently, that they would be involved in loss if they made advances for a period at a lower rate than would prevail at a time of tension.   Remove that sense of uneasiness when the reserve gets below a certain point, by the knowledge that there is a second reserve which can be utilised without any excessive cost, and the Bank of England will be helpless to protect its reserve: a vanishing process will commence, and eventually the second reserve will become the only reserve.

The amount of till money held by the banks is,

also, likely to be reduced by the introduction of
£1 notes. They could be transmitted far more
easily than gold from the country to London; and
banks in the country would be able to work with
a much leaner till. If they wanted to replenish
their till they could do so by means of the penny
post, whereas now the expense and the labour of
moving gold render a banker careful not to allow
his till money to run too low. Any drain
throughout the country would, therefore, concentrate itself upon the central reserve to a greater
extent than it does now, because of the smaller
amount of cash in the tills with which to meet it.

Mr. Goschen's proposal for the withdrawal of
the light coins—which he said is suspended because he thought it might be tacked on to larger
measures now in progress—is also calculated to
reduce the amounts held by the banks in their
tills. It sometimes suits a banker to retain light
gold in his till on the chance of putting it again
into circulation at an early date rather than sub-
mit to the loss on realisation at the Mint. When
the coinage is rehabilitated—which it is understood it will be at the expense of the State—it
will very often suit a banker to send a surplus to
the Mint, which he would not do now that he has

K

to bear the loss of the light weight. This, of course, is no reason why banks should not be relieved from the unfair loss they incur as last holders of the gold which has circulated; but it is necessary to bear in mind that the change will create an inducement to work with a smaller amount of till money, and consequently be the means of adding to the concentration upon the reserve at the centre.

The establishment of a second reserve, the introduction of £1 notes, and the rehabilitation of the gold coinage, are all calculated to increase the concentration upon the centre. Is it prudent of the Government to place the whole responsibility upon the discretion of the directors of the Bank of England? It does not seem to be a policy which would have commended itself to Sir Robert Peel. After the first breakdown of the Bank Charter Act in 1847 he said (on the 3rd Dec.):—
" I will now discuss the question whether there should be any modification of the Act of 1844. I think you ought to continue the restrictions of private and joint-stock banks. I think you ought to require of these banks to bear some share of the expense of keeping in reserve a stock of gold. I think, also, that if you do not impose the identi-

cal restrictions now imposed on the Bank of England, some restriction you must impose, for after the experience of 1826, 1836, and 1839, I, for one, am not content to leave the regulation of the monetary concerns of this country to the uncontrolled discretion of the Bank. In 1844 the general conviction was that it should not be so left; and I, for one, know no better mode of imposing restriction than that which was devised by the Act of 1844." Of course, Sir Robert Peel was discussing the question of again leaving the regulation of the issue of bank notes to the uncontrolled discretion of the Bank ; but having regard to the language he employed in expressing his opinion on that subject, it does not seem likely that he would be willing to create a second reserve of gold, and give the Bank an uncontrolled discretion to issue notes upon it. Since then there have been the catastrophes of 1857 and 1866; and the Bank of England has lost the control over the market which it formerly exercised. Would Sir Robert Peel, with the further experience of 1857 and 1866, place the second reserve in the uncontrolled discretion of the directors of one Institution—an Institution whose power in the market has diminished, is diminishing, and will diminish?

Moreover, there is no connection between the amount to be realised by means of an issue of £1 notes, and the total amount of the banks' deposits on account of which it is to form a second reserve. The amount so realised may remain stationary for years to come, whilst the amount of the banks' deposits may largely increase. There is no possibility of a sliding-scale between the two. A more natural proposal would be to create a second reserve by requiring all the banks to contribute towards it a certain proportion of their deposits; and this seems to be the meaning of the suggestion Sir Robert Peel made in the above quotation " I think you ought to require of these banks (the private and joint-stock banks) to bear some share of the expense of keeping in 'reserve a stock of gold."

A reserve created by requiring all the banks to contribute towards it a certain proportion of their deposits, would avoid the sacrifice Mr. Goschen said the State would incur in carrying out his proposals. He said:—" I have now indicated a method by which I think it (the amount of bullion) might be increased, and might be increased without imposing any tax on any portion of the community, but it would be secured by the State foregoing a portion of the profit which it would make upon the fiduciary issue. A certain amount of gold would be lying idle, and men would say ' Why should that gold remain idle ? ' 'What a sacrifice! Why is it so?' Well, it would be the State which would have foregone a portion of the profit which it made on the fiduciary issue, and it could say, ' It is of such enormous importance there should be a larger reserve of bullion in the country that we have foregone this profit which we may have made upon our paper issues because we believe it to be better to secure a reserve to which in times of crisis you may apply.' The alternative proposal of a second reserve created by requiring all the banks to contribute towards it a certain proportion of their deposits would avoid this sacrifice, and would place the burden upon the proper shoulders to bear it, viz., the proprietors of the banks."

CHAPTER VII.

A BANKING RESERVE.

MR. GOSCHEN referred to the question of compelling the banks to reserve a certain proportion of their deposits as follows:—" Now .in America there is a limitation imposed upon private bankers which is of a very remarkable character. The national banks are obliged to hold 25 per cent. in reserve against their deposits. Those are the issuing banks, it is true, but the State has considered that it is so important that those banks shall meet all their liabilities that it has imposed an iron limit of 25 per cent., and the banks are compelled to hold 25 per cent. in reserve against their deposits. I am bound to say that I should never propose such an iron system upon the great banking institutions of this country; but I mention it to show what in a free country such as America they do. The question of the proportion of deposits to liabilities was so serious that they introduced a cast-iron system. Then there were other suggestions, that if there was an excess of deposits and liabilities, up beyond a certain line, then that should be done which is done in some foreign lands, they should have to pay a certain tax upon the excess of their deposits. I will not say what view I hold upon such a suggestion, but in the most friendly spirit I would indicate to the banks of this country that the public have an enormous interest in the proportion of the reserve which they hold to deposits."

The iron system of America is certainly not worthy of imitation. The essential idea of a reserve is that it can be utilised when required, and to say that a bank shall not touch a certain portion of its funds under any circumstances, is a most unreasonable lock up of its resources. Mr. Goschen will not do that. And with regard to the other suggestion it would be of little benefit to the public if banks were taxed if they did not keep a certain proportion of reserve to liabilities, unless it was made a condition that their reserves were not to become deposits in another bank. The filtering process, explained in a previous chapter, would destroy the effect of such a tax, as only a residuum of the amount received by that means would find its way to the ultimate reserve of unemployed cash.

But these two methods of securing a certain proportion of cash reserve to liabilities do not exhaust all the means of obtaining the end in view. That end, I take it, so far as the Government is chiefly concerned, is to see that such an amount of cash is kept in reserve as shall not render it again necessary for the Government to interfere with the ordinary law of the country in order to find ready money for banks who have undertaken liabilities which they are unable to discharge without such extraneous assistance : to protect itself from again being placed in the position of having to authorise a violation of the law under the threat of physical force (see Mr. Glyn's speech, p. 33).

To attain this end it would not be necessary to enquire into the nature of the respective liabilities of the banks, or to attempt to lay down a hard and fast line as to what would be a proper proportion of cash reserve to liabilities in every case. All that it would be necessary to enforce would be the setting aside of a *minimum* proportion of cash reserve to liabilities towards an insurance fund against the evils of excessive competition.

Taking the deposits of the banks, exclusive of those of the Bank of England, at the

amount quoted in Mr. Goschen's speech, viz.,
£600,000,000 to £620,000,000, and adding
thereto the amount of the Bank of England's
liabilities, say £40,000,000, there is a total of
£650,000,000. To this Sir John Lubbock would
add the amount of the Savings Banks deposits.
Speaking at the annual general meeting of the
London Chamber of Commerce on the 23rd March
he said :—"The Chancellor of the Exchequer had
expressed an earnest wish that banks kept a larger
reserve of gold. This was a point on which he
would like to apply to Mr. Goschen the same
arguments which the right hon. gentleman had
applied to joint-stock banks. Mr. Goschen, as
Chancellor of the Exchequer, was the greatest
banker in the country. The Government held
on behalf of the Savings Banks deposits amounting to £107,000,000, and he was glad to see that
they were continually tending to increase. How
much cash, however, had the Government in
hand against this enormous liability ? About
£500,000, or less than $\frac{1}{2}$ per cent. Let the
Government themselves act on their own advice,
and the thing was done. Example, they all
knew, was better than precept, and he had more
than once pointed out that in the absence of any

reserve in the case of the Savings Banks the Government set a bad example. He knew that there were circumstances in which deposits in Savings Banks differed from deposits in other banks, but they must remember that deposits were left with the Post Office by the less well-informed class, and it was quite possible to argue, from another point of view, that the Government, in connection with the Savings Banks deposits, ought to hold larger reserves. No doubt it might be said that, though the Government had little cash against the Savings Banks' deposits, they held an immense sum in Government securities. But so did other banks. They also had large investments in Government securities which, in all ordinary circumstances, were at once practically reserve. They were, however, dealing with what might happen in extraordinary circumstances." Mr. Bagehot in "Lombard Street," raised the same question (p. 330):—"I suppose almost everyone thinks that our system of Savings Banks is sound and good. Almost everyone will be surprised to hear that there is any possible objection to it. Yet see what it amounts to. By the last return the Savings Banks—the old and the Post Office together—contain about £60,000,000 of deposits, and against this they hold in the funds, securities of the best kind. But they hold no cash whatever. They have, of course, the petty cash about the various branches necessary for daily work. But of cash in ultimate reserve —cash in reserve against a panic—the Savings Banks have not a sixpence. These banks depend on being able in a panic to realise their securities. But it has been shown over and over again, that in a panic such securities can only be realised by the help of the Bank of England—that it is only the Bank with the ultimate cash reserve which has at such moments any new money, or any power to lend and act. If in a general panic there were a run on the Savings Banks, those banks could not sell £100,000 of Consols without the help of the Bank of England; not holding themselves a cash reserve for times of panic, they are entirely dependent on the one Bank which does hold that reserve."

This argument is of a purely theoretical character. It is all very well for Sir John Lubbock to say "they were dealing with what might happen in extraordinary circumstances." But facts are against him. Under no extraordinary circumstances which have ever arisen has there been a run upon

the Post Office Savings Banks.   But this cannot
be said of the other banks.   The proposal to establish a second reserve is not made with a view
to emergencies which have never occurred, but
to provide against evils which have been experienced in the past, and which in all probability
will recur in the future.   The Savings Banks do
not trade as the other banks do; they are banks
of investment; and they have been in no way
associated with the difficulties of the past, either
as causing them, or adding to them when they
have occurred.   They have never required a
reserve of cash to fall back upon in time of panic,
nor to realise their securities, because of any
extra demands made upon them ; and there is no
reason to apprehend that they ever will.   There
is an essential distinction between the business
of the Savings' Banks, and of the other banks,
which the public have always appreciated.

Moreover, the deposits of the banks and the
deposits of the Savings Banks are not on all-fours.
The liability is of an essentially different character.   In a time of panic there could not be a run
on the Savings Bank in the same way as has
happened in the case of the other banks.   Under
the Act 24 Vic. cap. 14, sec. 3, it is sufficient if

the demand for repayment is complied with within a period of ten days from the day on which it is made. In the case of the other banks most of their liabilities are payable on demand. Cash reserves are required to meet sudden and unexpected demands payable at once, not to meet demands payable in the future. And the $\frac{1}{2}$ per cent. of cash reserve held by the Savings Banks against deposits not repayable until after the expiration of ten days' notice, is a more potent reserve than the 13 per cent. of the London and Westminster Bank against liabilities of which the repayment of a large portion can be required at a moment's notice.

For these reasons it would not be fair to expect the Savings Banks to contribute to the proposed banking reserve.

Sir John Lubbock also said, " It must also be remembered that, besides the English joint-stock and private banks, there were the large and numerous foreign and colonial banks which were established here. They also held very large deposits, and it might be said that it would be unfair to touch one set of banks and not another set." If these banks accept the responsibility of deposits repayable in London on demand, they should certainly be called upon to contribute to the central reserve proportionately. But these would not be large figures.

Without taking the deposits of the Savings Banks, or the deposits payable on demand in London of the foreign and colonial banks, into account, the total liabilities of the Bank of England and the other banks are estimated at £650,000,000. Of this amount there are no means of forming a reliable estimate of the proportion which the deposits payable on demand bear to those payable after notice. If those figures were forthcoming it would be better for the purpose of creating a central reserve, to base the calculation of the amount to be reserved upon the amount of the liabilities payable on demand, rather than the total amount of the liabilities. These particulars could be required. In the absence of those figures, it will be observed that a percentage of $2\frac{1}{2}$ per cent. of the total liabilities of £650,000,000 would produce a cash reserve of £16,250,000, which is substantially larger than the reserve of the Banking Department of the Bank of England. In this way a second reserve of £16,250,000 in cash would be created, and if safe notes were issued upon it (as Mr. Goschen suggests shall be done with the second reserve he proposes to create by means of an issue of £1 notes) the total amount of available money would be largely increased. But the proposal to call into existence two classes of bank notes—one issued upon the cash reserve in the Issue Department, and the other upon the second reserve—is open to serious objection. And as a second reserve of £16,250,000 would, probably, be ample it is not worth while to discuss any currency schemes by which it could be increased.

The custodians of this banking reserve could be the Bank of England. The Bank now acts "as managers on behalf of the public of the circulation of the country,"* upon lines laid down by the Bank Charter Act 1844, and the Bank in a similar way could be appointed the managers on behalf of the public of the banking reserve of the country.

The first condition to be imposed would be that the banking reserve should be kept wholly apart from the ordinary business of the Bank of England. It would frustrate the object of the creation of the second reserve if it was employed,

---

* See the letter of the Chancellor of the Exchequer of the 26th April, 1844, quoted on p. 44.

as the "bankers' balances" are now, in the ordinary business of the Bank. It should be a reserve which would only be utilised in extraordinary emergencies—such as have hitherto been met by the suspension of the Bank Charter Act. And the Government should make a similar provision as to the rate of interest to be charged when it is made use of as they have done when a suspension of the Act has been authorised. The last time the Government authorised a suspension of the Act, on the 11th May, 1866,* they wrote: —"If the directors of the Bank of England, proceeding upon the prudent rules of action by which their administration is usually governed, shall find that, in order to meet the wants of legitimate commerce, it be requisite to extend their discounts and advances upon approved securities, so as to require issues of notes beyond the limits fixed by law, her Majesty's Government recommend that this necessity should be met immediately upon its occurrence, and in that event they will not fail to make application to Parliament for its sanction. No such discount or advance, however, should be granted at a rate

---

* See Appendix C.

of interest less than 10 per cent., and her Majesty's government reserve it to themselves to recommend, if they should see fit, the imposition of a higher rate. After deduction by the Bank of whatever it may consider to be a fair charge for its risk, expense, and trouble, the profits of these advances will accrue to the public."

A charge of 10 per cent. per annum would be sufficient to protect the second reserve from use upon ordinary occasions. It would be an expensive luxury. At the same time the knowledge that this reservoir could be made use of at any time, without the special sanction of the Government being first required, might lead to a greater reliance being placed upon it than is now placed upon the suspension of the Act. To some extent, therefore, the establishment of a second reserve might, perhaps, reduce the amount of the present reserves of banks. But the penalty of a 10 per cent. rate of interest would probably be sufficient to prevent any very appreciable diminution in the first lines of defence. If, however, experience showed that it was not, the rate of interest to be charged could be increased until it became sufficiently penal to arrest any tendency in that direction; or the second reserve could be

L

increased by requiring a larger contribution to it.

The next point for consideration is the security which should be required for advances made out of this fund. It would be improper to require any security for the amount which stood to the credit of any bank. They ought to pay interest for its use as a penalty for overtrading, but, after all, the money deposited as an insurance fund would form a portion of their assets (which should be returned in the event of their discontinuing business), and they should not be required to furnish security for the use of their own money. But if an advance was required from the banking reserve what security should be obtained ? It will have been observed that when the Government authorised the suspension of the Act it was left to the discretion of the directors of the Bank of England to " extend their discounts and advances upon approved securities." The difficulty with regard to discounts would be the making a distinction between the different classes of paper offered for discount, and although it has existed when the Act has been suspended, yet it would be better to avoid it if practicable. With regard to " approved securities " they could

be limited to those Stock Exchange securities which
are approved by the Trust Investment Act, 1889,
and a margin of say 15 per cent. be required.

But what would be the probable demand upon
the banking reserve for advances at 10 per cent.
interest? If the experience afforded by the
suspension of the Bank Charter Act is a fair
criterion—and there is no reason why it should
not be—of what may be expected to happen, there
will most likely be no applications for assistance.
After the suspensions of the Act in 1847 and
1866, the demands for ready money immediately
ceased, and no extra issue of notes was required;
and the only time the "legal" limit was exceeded
—in 1857—the amount was only about £447,000.
The knowledge that money could be obtained at
a price was sufficient to stop the demand for it.
The fear lest no sacrifice would be enough to
obtain ready money in time to meet the payment
of liabilities becoming due was removed, and
with it the motive to hoard. It may, therefore,
be reasonably anticipated that the establishment
of a second reserve will prevent the possibility
of a recurrence of " Black Friday." Anxiety
could not reach the acute stage so long as there
is a sufficiently large available reservoir to fall

back upon in a time of crisis; and although the loss in interest might be serious, yet, with the removal of the principal cause which intensifies panic, it is not to be supposed that the sacrifice involved in a 10 per cent. interest would produce any great excitement.

With the money market in a comparatively reasonable frame of mind it would not be necessary to use the banking reserve for the discount of bills. Provided the banks have a store of unused cash to resort to, out of which advances could be made upon first-class Stock Exchange securities, it would not be necessary to resort to that fund for the discount of bills. The banks would have no fear in making their ordinary advances and discounts if they knew they could sell or obtain money upon good Stock Exchange securities—of which they hold a large amount. Some banks might, perhaps, have a certain delicacy in pledging their securities, and it would be better, therefore, to make the second reserve available for anyone who produced the required security, so that the banks might be supplied indirectly by means of the brokers. The importance of doing so would be to make it as easy as possible for banks to adopt a bold policy in a time of crisis instead of the policy of hoarding which they now instinctively adopt. In times of emergency the " bankers' balances " always largely increase, because they fear to make their ordinary advances, and consequently they promote the sense of uneasiness ; whereas, if they pursued their ordinary methods of business, they would not be the means of spreading apprehension. At one time it seemed as if the situation created by the Baring crisis might have been seriously complicated because some of the banks were exhibiting a tendency to hoard. Such a policy at such a time is utterly indefensible. The time to accumulate is before the storm arises; afterwards it is folly. However, with a large reservoir of available cash to fall back upon the banks generally would no longer have the same reason for timidity, and they may be expected to act as they did in the recent crisis.

It may be objected that if anyone is granted advances on securities from the second reserve it might possibly be drained, and the banks would not be able to withdraw their deposits if they wished to do so. A similar objection might be made to the whole system of banking, and it might be said " if banks were suddenly called upon to pay up all their balances they could not possibly do so,"—to which Mr. Rowland Hamilton would reply " Just so ! And if every man in London were suddenly to insist on laying up three months' store of provisions in his own house, there would certainly be famine till people recovered their senses." It is inconceivable that with a second reserve of £16,500,000 available to anyone who produces proper security on paying 10 per cent. interest there should be a considerable demand upon it. The existence of such a reserve would prevent any demand for money arising from panic ; and its being open to all, instead of only to the banks, would be the means of lessening, not increasing, the risk of any drain upon it.

The question of remuneration for the management of the banking reserve is not a difficult matter. In the event of any advances being required the interest of 10 per cent. would supply the means, and give a surplus. On the other hand, if there were no demands for advances the work would be very little. An annual statement by each bank of the amount of its liabilities, and a remittance of the required percentage, would be all that would be necessary. A reserve of the character proposed need not bear an exact proportion of cash to liabilities. So long as it grew from year to year with the growth of the banking deposits the principle involved would be fairly carried out. For the first year it might be advisable only to make a call for half the percentage which would be required, in order that the operation might not cause any great inconvenience to the market.

With regard to the attitude which the banks generally would take towards a proposal for a banking reserve, they would, probably, prefer to see a reserve established which would be administered upon certain definite lines, than one intrusted to the uncontrolled discretion of the Bank of England, so that it could "come to the rescue of the mercantile community generally." The contribution to the central reserve of $2\frac{1}{2}$ per cent. of their liabilities—which would still form a portion of their assets, and which they could at any time utilise on payment of 10 per cent. interest— would be a trifling matter. And if they reduced their balances with their agents, or the Bank of England as the case may be, to that extent, and the Bank of England retained the same proportion of reserve to liabilities as it now does, the effect upon the reserve of the Bank of England —the only existing store of unused cash—would be very slight. The retention of so small a proportion as $2\frac{1}{2}$ per cent. of the liabilities of a well-conducted bank by the central reserve, instead of keeping all their reserve (or balance) at their agents, or the Bank of England, would not affect their profits, and they would secure immunity from the losses and risks resulting from panic.

The well-conducted banks would also be glad to see the establishment of a second reserve in view of the difficulty referred to by Mr. Goschen as follows:—"The public have an enormous interest in the proportion of the reserves which the banks hold to deposits. They all hold together; and you have this remarkable fact, that the soundest and strongest banks may be making the smallest dividends, whilst the more imprudent banks, who invest the depositors' money, leaving a small reserve, are able to show much larger dividends to their shareholders. Why are the latter able to take this course? Because they have the conviction that the failure of any one of these big banks would be such a disaster to the whole

community that the other banks would be compelled to come to their assistance, and to rescue
the offending bank from the consequence of its
offences by themselves undertaking a part of
their liabilities. The more imprudent banks will
say, ' There is no imprudence. We shall never
be allowed to fail; our fellow bankers must come
to our assistance, and, if not our fellow bankers,
then the Bank of England ; and, if not the Bank
of England, then the Government.' " In the
event of a second reserve being established the
well-conducted banks, who keep a fair and proper
proportion of reserve to liabilities, will not find
their good management neutralised by badly
managed banks ; and the imprudent banks will
learn that the market is strong enough to let
them go.

The establishment of a second reserve would,
moreover, be a great boon to the mercantile
community. The defect which the Governor of
the Bank of England perceives in the existing
system of finance would, to a large extent, be
remedied. He said (see p. 87) :—" The principle of the existing system of finance in this
country is a very good one. The only question
that has been raised is, whether under competi-

tion and in the pursuit of economy, it has not been pushed a little further than is consistent with the interests of trade and commerce. Where reserves are small, any 'pull' upon them by withdrawals to foreign countries necessarily makes a large reduction in our reserve, and, as I have already explained, as that reserve is practically the reserve of the country, the reduction has a much larger effect upon the value of money than it would have if the balances were larger." The sensitiveness of the market when a "pull" takes place would not be so keen if there was a second reserve of available cash. The supply of money could be increased at any time on payment of 10 per cent. interest, and if withdrawals continued the value of money would gradually level up to that amount; but there would be no unreasonable increase in the value of money as sometimes now arises from dread of a scarcity, and the uncertainty as to how far matters might proceed until the Government saw fit to authorise a suspension of the Act. The mercantile community would no longer be subject to the inconvenience occasioned by banks suddenly discontinuing their ordinary advances; and although, if the first reserves were generally allowed to be unduly diminished, they might have to pay a stiff price for the accommodation, yet it could be obtained.

A reserve so created would be the means of placing the burden of maintaining a stock of unused cash upon the shoulders of the proper persons to bear it, viz., those who undertake to pay large sums on demand; it would grow *pari passu* with the growth of those liabilities ; and it would add to the existing stock of gold in this country. On the other hand, Mr. Goschen's proposal to establish a second reserve by means of an issue of £1 notes is to sacrifice the profits of the issue which belong to the community as a whole for the benefit of a section thereof; to establish a fund which has no relation to the purpose for which it is required, and which has no elasticity to meet the growing demands of the future; and to draw upon the stock of gold circulating in the country—not for any national emergency such as a great war *—but for the purpose of carrying on the ordinary business of the country.

---

* Mr. Weguelin, the Governor of the Bank of England in 1856, wrote to the Chancellor of the Exchequer that "It should be the policy of the Legislature to encourage the circulation of coin for small payments, and prohibit the use of £1 and £2 notes. This would be a reserve in times of extreme difficulty." (See Appendix B).

CHAPTER VIII.

CONCLUSION.

THE speech which Mr. Goschen delivered at Leeds has been republished, and in a preface he says:—"On one topic alone of those touched in my speech I should like to say one word of explanation, or rather of correction. I find that the way in which I expressed myself as to devising possible precautions against panics, and as to the establishment of larger reserves, side by side with remarks on the 'Baring crisis,' has led to some misapprehension. I did not mean that, if financial houses undertook liabilities on too gigantic a scale, any banking or currency precautions could prevent disastrous results, especially to themselves. But I intended to call attention to the fact that the catastrophe might have been vastly aggravated to others from the existence of too small aggregate reserves in the hands of the banking and financial world to meet such a crisis. I wished to emphasise the 'unpreparedness,' in my judgment, of the banking world to meet a

strain even less than that which so extraordinary
an event as the straits of the great house in
question brought about. Some of my critics
have said: 'Such an abnormal event can never
occur again.' But even if this were granted, it
seems to me nevertheless to be true that the
lesson of insufficient reserves and insufficient
stock of gold, taught the country in November
last, is none the less of the deepest importance,
as it is applicable to many panics and times of
difficulty falling far short of the extreme danger
revealed on this particular occasion."

The difficulties of the "Baring crisis" were
great because of the magnitude of the firm's
operations; but there were circumstances connected with it which reduced it to much smaller
proportions than the crisis the money market
would be called upon to go through in the event
of the failure of one of the large London joint-
stock banks. When those institutions were,
comparatively, in their infancy, Mr. Weguelin,
the Governor of the Bank of England, drew the
attention of the Chancellor of the Exchequer to
the danger to the credit of the country in
consequence of the smallness of their reserves,
remarking that it was "impossible to foresee the

consequences of the failure of one of these large establishments; and it is a branch of the subject which in my opinion more pressingly requires the attention of Parliament than any alteration in the Bank Acts of 1844 and 1845." (Mr. Weguelin's letter of 10 November, 1856, see Appendix B.) Thus, in Mr. Weguelin's opinion, the attention of Parliament was pressingly required thirty-five years ago to the dangers to the community, which would arise in the event of the failure of one of the large joint-stock banks, in consequence of the smallness of their reserves. Since then the business of those institutions has enormously increased, and the question more urgently requires to be faced. Mr. Goschen's critics who do not consider that provision should be made against the contingency of a repetition of the "Baring crisis," as "such an abnormal event can never occur again," should take into consideration the state of affairs, which would be produced with our present reserves if one of the large London joint-stock banks should fail. The "Baring crisis" was an extensive affair, but its effects were very much minimised by the fact of one of the members of the firm—a director of the Bank of England—supplying information which enabled

the Bank to import gold and to investigate the
firm's position before its troubles became public ;
and also by the fact that although its assets were
not of a readily realisable character, yet they
showed so substantial a surplus over liabilities
that the Bank felt justified in undertaking to pay
all liabilities as they became due, and in calling
upon the other banks to join in a guarantee
against ultimate loss. Such abnormally favourable
circumstances as those under which the " Baring
crisis " took place are not likely to occur again
when the next crisis comes. Furthermore, the
intensity of a crisis arising from the failure of
one of the joint-stock banks would be much
greater than was the case in the " Baring crisis "
since more people would be directly affected, and
the liabilities are of a more pressing character.
To give relief at such a time it would not only be
necessary to arrange for the payment of liabilities
to become due, but to at once grant accommodation to the customers whose money was locked
up in the bank which had failed, and who had to
meet liabilities then due. If this were not done
the crisis would extend, and the difficulties of the
situation would be enormously aggravated. A
" Baring crisis " compared to the crisis which

would occur in the event of the failure of one of
the large London joint-stock banks, with our
present cash reserves, is child's play.

But it may be said that in calling the attention
of the Government to what would happen in the
event of the failure of one of the large joint-stock
banks, Mr. Weguelin was contemplating an impossibility; or that if he was right then the
balance-sheets show their position now to be im-
pregnable. The balance-sheets of the City of
Glasgow Bank and the West of England and
South Wales District Bank were considered to
be highly satisfactory: the £100 shares of the
former, which paid a dividend of 12 per cent.,
stood at £235 10s. on the day before its failure,
as the balance-sheet had failed to reveal the fact
that the capital was all lost, and that every solvent
shareholder would not only lose what he gave for
his shares, but also would have to contribute
towards the deficiency after realisation £2,750
for every £100 share he held. It may be improb-
able that one of the large London joint-stock
banks should ever fail (although it is difficult to
understand why the magnitude of a bank's operations should lessen the chances of its mismanage-
ment); but there is the risk—which a sanguine

man will ignore, and a prudent one will provide against. If Parliament had taken the advice of the Governor of the Bank of England 35 years ago, and had adopted means to provide against the contingency of the failure of one of the large joint-stock banks, although the cash reserve would not have been required for that purpose, yet there would have been no crisis of 1857, and no "Black Friday" in 1866. Overend and Gurney would have failed, but they would not have dragged down several solvent people with them. The innocent would not have suffered with the guilty. What actually happened is described by Mr. Patterson in his "Science of Finance," p. 239 :—" Contemplate the magnitude of the disaster. Overend, Gurney and Co., the oldest and most powerful discount house in the Kingdom— the English Joint Stock Bank, which fell because a large portion of its deposits was locked up in the stoppage of Overend and Co.—the Imperial Mercantile Credit Co., the European Bank, the Bank of London, the Consolidated Bank, and the Agra and Masterman's, with its wide-spread connections, were wrecked during that terrible season of panic. All three—the Bank of London, the Consolidated Bank, and the Agra and Master-

M

man's—were perfectly solvent establishments;
the two latter subsequently resumed business.
Their suspension (which was only momentary in
the case of the Consolidated Bank) was caused
not by a want of assets, but the impossibility of
converting their assets into currency (Bank of
England notes), in order to meet the unusual
demand upon them." If Mr. Weguelin's advice
had been taken, and Parliament had then established an available second reserve these solvent
banks would not have had to suspend payments;
and their customers would not have experienced
great, and undeserved, trouble.

The miseries which follow a great panic are
apt to be forgotten in times of prosperity. They
cannot better be described than they were by
Miss Martineau in 1846 when writing of the consequences resulting from the panic of 1825:—
" There are many now living who remember that
year with bitter pain. They saw parents grow
white-haired in a week's time; lovers parted on
the eve of marriage; light-hearted girls sent forth
from home as governesses or sempstresses; governesses, too old for new situations, going actually
into the workhouse; rural gentry quitting their
lands; and whole families relinquishing every

prospect in life, and standing as bare under the storm as Lear and his strange comrades upon the heath!"

The establishment of a second reserve is not to be regarded as a panacea against all the evils resulting from incapacity. So long as the conduct of large and important undertakings is liable to fall into the hands of too sanguine and incompetent men, there will always be a recurrence of difficulty and distress. But those evils may be minimised, and confined within narrower limits, by the strengthening of the cash reserves upon which the well-managed institutions can fall back in a time of stress. A second reserve will remedy that "unpreparedness" of the banking world, which Mr. Goschen emphasises, to meet a strain even less than that which so extraordinary an event as the straits of the Barings brought about; and it should be sufficiently large to enable the market to cope with the difficulties in which it would be involved in the event of the failure of one of the large joint-stock banks. That standard for the market to arrive at, which Mr. Weguelin set up thirty-five years ago, viz.:—to be sufficiently strong to be able to face the danger to others of the failure of one of the large joint-stock banks is not too high: nothing less will satisfy the dictates of prudence that dominate the mercantile community.

As the "unpreparedness" of the banking world is to be attributed in the first place to the monopoly of "exclusive banking" granted to the Bank of England; resulting in its now being an open question whether the Bank keeps a reserve to supply its own requirements or whether it is keeping a reserve to supply the needs of all the banks; and to an indifference as to the consequences because of an improper reliance upon the Government to come to the rescue of the banking community when it gets into a difficulty by sanctioning a violation of the law; it is preeminently a matter for Parliament to deal with.

APPENDIX A.

THE following Paper was prepared by Mr. Freshfield for the information of the Chancellor of the Exchequer in Nov., 1856, and opposite is inserted what appears to be a conclusive reply.

The question now asked is, whether, in case of the insolvency of the Bank of England, the holders of Bank notes would have any right of payment out of the bullion, and securities held by the Bank in the Issue Department, in preference to the depositors?

MR. FRESHFIELD.	REPLY.
1. It is certain that no such preference existed before the passing of Sir Robert Peel's Act. Did that Act give such preference?	1. Yes.
2. That Act was not passed with any view to the rights of creditors. The object is to regulate the circulation, and limit the issue of Bank notes.	2. Section 2 of the Act states :—And the whole amount of Bank of England notes then in circulation, including those delivered to the Banking Department as aforesaid, shall be deemed to be issued on the credit of such securities, coin and bullion so appropriated and set apart to the Issue Department.
3. That limit is ascertained by the amount of bullion in the Issue Department.	3. *Plus* the securities.
4. By the operation of the Act, the Bank cannot withdraw bullion from the Issue Department without reducing the notes in circulation *pro tanto*.	4. Certainly.
5. The effect of this is, that the Bank can pay the bullion in the Issue Department to none but note holders.	5. Certainly.
6. Conceding, therefore, that while the Bank continues its operations the provisions of the Act do operate to give a preference to the note holders, would they have a preference in case the Bank were wound up in bankruptcy.	6. Yes. The securities, coin and bullion are specially set apart and appropriated for the payment of the notes by section 2, quoted above.
7. It may be argued, that the provisions of the Act would remain, and that bullion could be taken only from the Issue Department in payment of notes.	7. Certainly.

MR. FRESHFIELD.	REPLY.
8. Or, that the circulation being at an end, the provisions of the Act will no longer apply.	8. Circulation not necessarily at an end. The Issue Department is entirely independent of the Banking Department, and is carried on in a separate building.
9. I apprehend the last is the true view of the law.	9. Join issue.
10. That the provisions of the Act are not for the benefit of the note holders, but for ascertaining the limit of issue, is clear, not only from the general policy of the Act, but from the contemporaneous enactments as to banks in Scotland and Ireland, where the issue is equally limited by the amount of bullion without any provisions that could tend to secure that bullion to the note holders.	10. Section 2 as quoted above specially sets apart and appropriates the securities, coin and bullion, in the Issue Department for the benefit of the note holders.
11. In fact, the provisions of the Act in question are not applicable to a liquidation, and no rights of preference being given by the Act but those flowing only from its provisions, if these latter fail the consequent preference fails.	11. Why not applicable to a liquidation? Section 2 does give rights of preference.
12. If the Bank were bankrupt, the bullion being less by 14,000,000 than the notes out, the bullion could no longer be issued under the provisions of the Act in exchange for notes without creating a preference among the note holders, or rather a scramble, and therefore must be distributed rateably either to the note holders or to all the creditors.	12. This is assuming that the securities set apart and appropriated for payment of the notes are not realisable. The directors of the Bank as " managers on behalf of the public of the circulation of the country " (see letter of the Chancellor of the Exchequer quoted in note on p. 44) if a great demand for the payment of the notes arose would take steps to realise the securities before a scramble could take place; and as Sir Robert Peel said, in reply to a question of Mr. Muntz on the 6th January, 1844: " If the 11 millions of Government debt should be required by the Bank, the Government would have no difficulty in raising the amount to pay it off."

13. Such a distribution would in neither case be in accordance with any provisions of the Act. As there could be no distribution founded on the provisions of the Act, another rule must be sought, and I conceive the creditors must be remitted to their legal rights.

13. Such a distribution would not be necessary unless it is assumed that the Government could not pay its debt, and the remainder of the securities could not be realised—which is not asserted. Sec. 2 states " It shall be lawful for the said Governor and Co. to diminish the amount of such securities, and so from time time as they shall see occasion."

14. Now, it is clear, that if a body carries on two businesses and becomes bankrupt, the funds of both become a common fund, and all creditors rank rateably. This was decided in the case of Strahan, Paul and Co., who had a bank and a navy agency house, carried on with different funds in different houses, and under different names, but in bankruptcy the assets of both were thrown into one common fund.

14. The securities are set apart and legally appropriated to the note holders, who are thus secured creditors.

15. But it is submitted, that the question sought to be raised is of no practical importance, and tends to raising unnecessary apprehension. It may be that the division of accounts renders the administration of the Bank difficult. It is not necessary to discuss that point; the objection implied in the question is, that the Bank would in an ultimate liquidation be less solvent in its banking department, which is a mischievous insinuation.

15. The practical importance of the subject arises from the necessity of investigating the claims on the Bank, because of its relation with the Government in connection with the issue of notes.

16 The credit of the Bank is not and never has been in doubt. It would be unwise to raise such a question if there were a doubt. It is still more so in the actual state of things.

16. Certainly.

17. The risk to be apprehended is a drain of gold. Under such a drain, the Bank has stopped payment heretofore with little or no bullion in its coffers, but without the slightest discredit, and it is not likely to be now discredited if it should stop payment with 3,000,000 or 4,000,000 of gold in its coffers.

17. The Banking Department is subject to the law of Bankruptcy. Special permission not to pay in cash was given by the Government in 1797, but it was refused in 1825.

18. Nor is it likely that discredit should arise from the state of the deposit accounts. Everyone knows that the Bank has ample means to meet its deposits. The argument that the small amount of notes in reserve tends to discredit the Bank in the Banking Department is an argument against publication, or against the limit of issue, and not against the appropriation of gold in the Issue Department.

18. The argument that the small amount of notes in reserve tends to discredit the Bank in the Banking Department is not an argument against publication, nor against the limit of issue : it is an argument in favour of increasing the amount of notes in reserve in the Banking Department, which is now better understood and acted upon. It is certainly no argument in favour of appropriating the gold in the Issue Department to supply any deficiency of the Banking Department.

19. Assuming, therefore, the extreme case of a suspension, the difficulty would not be the discredit of the Bank, but a want of circulating medium.

19. A suspension would certainly be the discredit of the Bank. The circulating medium is not a fixed quantity, but can always be increased by the purchase of gold, which can be exchanged for notes.

20. The Bank note circulation required by the public is about 20,000,000, and if the circulation were reduced to as low as 17,000,000 or 18,000,000, the Bank would still have 3,000,000 to 4,000,000 of gold.

20. The £3,000,000 or £4,000,000 would be in the Issue Department, specially set aside and appropriated for payment of the notes, and not available for the purposes of the Banking Department.

21. The Bank, by extreme pressure on the community, might get in and cancel even more notes. But before this the pressure on the community, from want of circulating medium, would be so severe as to produce universal suspension. The private banks would be stopped, and the whole exchange of the country at an end, and the mercantile community would be reduced to a state of barter.

21. Any of the large joint-stock banks could do the same, but that fact gives them no title to the gold in the Issue Department.

MR. FRESHFIELD.   REPLY.

22. To inquire, therefore, of the rights of the Bank creditors is futile. They are safe in any case, and the question resolves itself into that of the policy of limiting the issue of Bank notes, not of the security for the issue.

22. The question resolves itself into whether or not the holders of the notes are entitled to the securities, coin and bullion appropriated and set apart by the Act, on the credit of which they have been issued.

(Signed)   JAMES FRESHFIELD, Jun.
24th November, 1856.

Appendix to report from the select committee on the Bank Acts. Appendix No. 17.

Papers of the House of Commons.   Session 1857-8 v. 5, pp. 427-428.

APPENDIX B.

REMARKS and opinions of the Governors and some of the Directors of the Bank of England on the Bank Charter Act of 1844, and the Irish and Scotch Banking Acts of 1845.

QUESTIONS PROPOSED.

1. Have you any suggestion to offer with reference to the operation of the Act of 1844 ?

2. Would you recommend its renewal, as it stands, for another term ?

3. If not, what amendments to you seem advisable ?

NOTE.—I would beg of you to extend your observations to the Irish and Scotch Acts of 1845.

The Governor of the Bank of England to the Right Hon. the Chancellor of the Exchequer.

Bank of England, 10th *November,* 1856.

MY DEAR SIR GEORGE,—

I have the pleasure to forward to you copies of the opinions of several of my colleagues, upon the operation of the Banking Acts of 1844 and 1845, in reply to the desire expressed in your letter to me of the 24th September last.

In adding my own opinion, I am constrained to appeal to your indulgence if my remarks should acquire some length, though it will be my endeavour to indicate rather the heads of argument than to illustrate or develop them.

It appears to me that much of the opposition to the Act of 1844 has been directed rather against the reasoning upon which the Act was founded and by which it has been defended, than against the provisions of the Act itself. I am speaking, of course, of those who consider some limit beyond simple convertibility of the note as necessary.

If I consider the plan enunciated by Mr. Palmer, or the opinions of Mr. Tooke, I am led to the conclusion that they involve the idea of some such limit, although, in my opinion, not of so effective application as that established by the Act of 1844.

Mr. Palmer's plan, you may recollect, consisted in maintaining an average amount of banking securities, independent of the capital of the Bank, and allowing the bullion to fluctuate according to the wants of commerce.

Mr. Tooke, apparently, would place the limit, or rather, the binding obligation, upon the amount of bullion to be maintained.

Now, I think the limitation of the Act of 1844 is easier of application, acts in a more constant and regular manner by a clearer distinction of the liabilities of the Bank ; and, as regards Mr. Palmer's plan, is felt at an earlier period of a drain of the precious metals.

The restriction placed upon the country issuers has, I think, operated beneficially in maintaining the credit of that portion of the circulation ; the exceptions in comparison with former periods having been unimportant. But, on the other hand, the Act, and more especially the reasoning of its supporters, encourage a dangerous theory that the Bank of England in its banking department may, in all respects, act as would a private banker in the management of his deposits. It thus favours the competition with private money-lenders, which in periods of large deposits is apt to produce an unwarranted inflation of credit. In periods of a drain of bullion, it makes no distinction as to the causes of the drain. Its theory is, that the Bank should be governed in its action by the rate of interest out of doors, and that whenever it has the power to raise the rate of discount it should use it. But here no distinction is drawn between a drain for exports, which is the consequence of an inflation of credit, and a drain for the internal accommodation of the country, which may be caused by discredit, or which may merely represent the natural oscillation of the currency.

These two causes, in my opinion, require opposite treatment.

The limitation of issue, which in the former case is salutary by forcing the Bank to defend its treasure by action on the rate of interest or restriction in the discount of bills, in the latter case of internal discredit, would add to and intensify the difficulty; or, in the case of the natural oscillation of the currency, leads to erroneous conclusions in the public mind as to the true position of the bank in times of difficulty.

Again, there are times and circumstances in the external demand for treasure which may render the maintenance of the limit impossible; circumstances, I mean, over which no action of the Bank can exercise control. I allude to Government loans in a state of war. The Government is enabled to borrow on its stock to an amount, and at a rate of interest, which has no affinity to the rate of discount which the Bank may think it necessary to demand. Having made its contract for the loan, it can use the proceeds by exporting treasure for the payment of troops on foreign service, wholly irrespective of any action on the part of the Bank.

Now with regard to the oscillation of the internal circulation of the country, I may notice that there is, periodically, a demand for currency from the Scotch and Irish banks, which, whilst it produces a most sensible effect upon the Bank of England reserve, is uncontrollable by any action of the Bank. At certain periods of the year, especially after harvest, the demand for currency commonly greatly exceeds the authorised issue; and as the excess must be issued on gold deposited in certain specified places, that gold is withdrawn from the Bank reserve, to be again restored to it when the reflux of the currency of the Scotch and Irish banks takes place, which is usually in the months of December to March. The Scotch banks very generally exceed their authorised aggregate issue; but with the Irish banks, although the aggregate issue is not usually exceeded, yet it often happens that some are in excess, whilst others are under the authorised amount. But as each bank has to provide for its own excess, the demand on the London bullion reserve is as great as if the whole Irish circulation had gone beyond its limit.

The quarterly oscillation of the English circulation amounts to from £2,000,000 to £2,500,000 in notes, and probably from £500,000 to £800,000 in coin. There is also noticeable a weekly vibration of both notes and coin. These effects are produced by the payment of dividends, salaries, wages, &c., and the receipt on the other hand for revenue and the setting free of circulation by the gradual disbursements of the public.

I notice this ebb and flow of the circulation, to show how the proportion of bullion which guarantees the active circulation, may vary. For instance :—The active circulation at one time of the quarter is £18,000,000, at another £20,500,000 : as £14,500,000 are issued in securities, it follows that £3,500,000 is the bullion guarantee of £18,000,000, and £6,000,000 the bullion guarantee of £20,500,000, or a varying proportion of 19 and 29 per cent.

The banking reserve is acted upon disadvantageously in similar proportions ; as, practically speaking, it must be understood that the banking reserve is the balance of the total issue, after satisfying the wants of the public for circulation.

There is a practical embarrassment in the working of the present Act, during periods of declining rates of interest, caused by the agreements with the bankers named in the Schedule of the Act, and by the duty of the Bank towards its private customers. Instead of an allowance of 1 per cent. per annum on the amount of abandoned circulation, the Bank agrees to discount certain specified amounts at 1 per cent. below the Bank's minimum rate. It seems equitable, therefore, that the Bank should not fix its minimum materially above the value of money out of doors. But I think this leads to an unwholesome competition with other lenders.

These or similar defects would probably be incidental to any measure of limitation beyond mere convertibility. Some of them might be removed by absorbing all other issues of bank notes, but the effect of this would not in my opinion be in all cases a substitution of Bank of England notes for country circulation. Much capital would thereby be lost, that is, actual gold and silver must be substituted for notes now used in internal transactions.

Irrespective of theories upon the subject of the currency, what should be the policy of the Legislature with regard to it ?

The receipts and payments by Government would undoubtedly maintain the credit of a large amount of bank notes apart from, and independent of, a metallic basis. Experience alone could show what this amount might safely be, supposing there were but a single issuer.

In the present composite structure of the currency, this may be said to be indicated by the £14,500,000 issued on securities so far as the Bank of England is concerned. It cannot be the policy of the Legislature to encourage the issue of bank notes to the utmost extent that the credit of the issuer would keep in circulation. It would be most desirable, even if there were one sole issuer, that a metallic reserve should be maintained in the country, not alone for the purposes of internal credit, but for occasions of sudden exigencies, which might occasion and demand an external drain of the precious metals.

If this would be desirable when the Government should have all the profit of the circulation, it is still more so when the profit is distributed amongst private undertakings.

With this view it should be the policy of the Legislature to encourage the circulation of coin for small payments, and prohibit the use of £1 and £2 notes. This would be a reserve in times of extreme difficulty.

It may be said that this argument favours the limitation of a paper circulation to its exact equivalent in bullion. But besides that this would be an unnecessary sacrifice of capital, it must be considered that the complete disuse of a credit circulation would be a serious bar to its introduction in times of emergency, causing alarm, and thereby adding to the difficulty rather than relieving it. Two questions here suggest themselves :—1. Would it be desirable that the circulation should be issued by the Government? and 2. Should the functions of issue be separated from those of banking, by placing the former department in the hands of special Commissioners?

1st. I think that the Government should have nothing to do with the issue of bank notes, as it would be subjected to all the clamour and unpopularity which are engendered by financial and monetary crises. The circulation would not be free from political influence, for reasons of State might be pleaded for measures which would endanger the value and stability of property : and experience has shown that no Government hitherto has possessed this power that has not abused it. In times of emergency, discredit of the Government paper would enormously add to the difficulty.

Some of these reasons apply to the separation of the Issue Department from the Bank of England, and there are other reasons which render this inexpedient.

It would more apparently than at present reduce the Bank of England to the level of an ordinary joint-stock Bank ; and thus the strength which is derived from the Bank's intimate connection with the Government would be lost.

This connection is assumed by the public to exist notwithstanding the enactment of 1844—the theory of which denies all value to this connection ; and I think it is necessary to maintain this impression, so long as it is deemed advisable to publish the weekly accounts of the Liabilities and Assets of the Bank. The separation would, moreover, relieve the Bank of some portion of its responsibility, and would be an inducement to manage its banking business more nearly on the principle of an ordinary joint-stock bank, investing its deposits much more closely and shutting its doors when it was not convenient to discount.

By this the distinctive character of the Bank of England, as a bank of reserve, would be lost ; and it is questionable whether a monied corporation, with so large a capital as the Bank of England, relieved from such responsibility, and deprived of such character, might not have a dangerous influence on the money market.

If the Act be continued in its present shape, there would remain to be discussed the questions, whether the present amount issued upon securities is correctly fixed at £14,500,000 ? and secondly, whether there should be a machinery provided for the relaxation of the Act in cases of emergency or discredit ?

On the first question, arguing on the principle of the Act, that a certain proportion of the active circulation should be issued in gold ; I am inclined to think the amount should not be increased.

The circulation in the hands of the public varies from £18,000,000 to £21,000,000.

At the lowest point, the Act would require £3,500,000 ; at the highest, £6,500,000 in gold, as a basis to ensure convertibility. To raise the issue on securities to £16,000,000, as proposed by Mr. Norman, would reduce these bases respectively to £2,000,000 and £5,000,000, which appears to me too low a proportion.

Secondly, as to the power of relaxation. This point was fully considered by the framers of the Act. To provide machinery for the purpose of relaxing, it was thought, would encourage an undue reliance upon this exceptional means of relief, and that it was the function of the Government to intervene in such a case, and of the Government alone, under its official responsibility.

This power having been once exercised already, there is no cause to apprehend a panic, such as occurred in 1847. The public believe that it would be exercised again under similar circumstances. Some advantages might be derived, possibly, from an enactment, laying down rules how such power should be exercised. Having considered the question fully, as regards the limitation placed upon the power of issue, a large portion of the subject has not been adverted to, which relates to the management of the Bank of England, and, by implication, of other banks, as a bank of deposit.

And here the first anomaly that presents itself, and which is at the root of all the difficulty to which the Bank is subjected under any system of restriction, is that the Bank is expected to open its doors to all comers, and make advances to any amount, provided only good banking security, such as unexceptional bills of exchange, are tendered to it.

There are two ways of meeting the difficulty caused by this anomaly.

One is by successively raising the rate of interest, which, it is assumed, will eventually raise the value of money above its value abroad, and thus cause it to flow to this country ; the other is, by placing restriction upon the term for which the Bank makes advances, and thus acting directly on the Foreign exchanges by discouraging the negotiation of any but bills at short date upon England.

The Bank has of late, to a certain extent, combined these modes of action.

It is not here the place to enter upon arguments *pro.* and *con.* upon this subject; and I therefore pass on to the question as to the proportion of reserve which the Bank should endeavour to maintain in its Banking Department.

This is notoriously very much higher than any private banker deems necessary in the management of his deposits; and, according to the usual practice of the Bank, varies in times of scarcity of money, from one - third to one - fourth the amount of its deposits.

But if this be contrasted with the reserves kept, for instance, by the joint-stock banks, a new and hitherto little-considered source of danger to the credit of the country will present itself. The joint-stock banks of London, judging by their published accounts, have deposits to the amount of £30,000,000. Their capital is not more than £3,000,000, and they have on an average £31,000,000 invested in one kind of security or another, leaving only £2,000,000 of reserve against all this mass of liabilities.

It is impossible to forsee the consequences of a failure of one of these large establishments; and it is a branch of the subject which, in my opinion, more pressingly requires the attention of Parliament than any alteration in the Banking Acts of 1844 and 1845.

I remain, &c.,

(Signed)   T. M. WEGUELIN.

Appendix to report from the Select Committee on the Bank Acts, pp. 1-4.

Papers of the House of Commons, 1857, Sess. II., vol. 10, pt. II., Bank Acts.

APPENDIX C.

Letter of the First Lord of the Treasury and the Chancellor of the Exchequer authorising the suspension of the Bank Charter Act, 1844.

To the Governor and Deputy-Governor of the Bank of England.

Downing Street,
May 11th, 1866.

GENTLEMEN,—

We have the honour to acknowledge the receipt of your letter of this day to the Chancellor of the Exchequer, in which you state the course of action at the Bank of England, under the circumstances of sudden anxiety which have arisen since the stoppage of Messrs. Overend, Gurney, and Co., Limited, yesterday.

We learn with regret that the Bank reserve, which stood so recently as last night at a sum of about five millions and three quarters, has been reduced in a single day by the liberal answer of the Bank to the demands of commerce during the hours of business, and by its great anxiety to divert disaster, to little more than half that amount, or a sum (actual for London and estimated for the branches) not greatly exceeding three millions.

The accounts and representations which have reached Her Majesty's Government during the day, exhibit the state of things in the city as one of extraordinary distress and apprehension. Indeed, deputations composed of persons of the greatest weight and influence, and representing alike the private and joint-stock banks of London, have presented themselves in Downing Street, and have urged with unamimity, and with earnestness, the necessity of some intervention on the part of the State, to allay the anxiety which prevails, and which appears to have amounted, through great part of the day, to absolute panic.

There are some important points in which the present crisis differs from those of 1847 and 1857. Those periods were periods of mercantile distress, but the vital consideration of banking credit does not appear to have been involved in them, as it is in the present crisis.

Again, the course of affairs was comparatively slow and measured, whereas the shock has in this instance arrived with an intense rapidity, and the opportunity for deliberation is narrowed in proportion. Lastly, the reserve of the Bank of England has suffered a diminution without precedent relatively to the time in which it has been brought about, and in view especially of this circumstance Her Majesty's Government cannot doubt that it is their duty to adopt, without delay, the measures which seem to them best calculated to compose the public mind, and to arrest the calamities which may threaten trade and industry. If, then, the directors of the Bank of England, proceeding upon the prudent rules of action by which their administration is usually governed, shall find that, in order to meet the wants of legitimate commerce, it be requisite to extend their discounts and advances upon approved securities, so as to require issue of notes beyond the limits fixed by law, Her Majesty's Government recommend that this necessity should be met immediately upon its occurrence, and in that event they will not fail to make application to Parliament for its sanction.

No such discount or advance, however, should be granted at a rate of interest less than 10 per cent., and Her Majesty's Government reserve it to themselves to recommend, if they should see fit, the imposition of a higher rate. After deduction by the Bank of whatever it may consider to be a fair charge for its risk, expense, and trouble, the profits of these advances will accrue to the public.

We have the honour to be, gentlemen,

Your obedient servants,

RUSSELL.

W. E. GLADSTONE.

CATALOGUE

OF

COMMERCIAL AND OTHER WORKS

PUBLISHED AND SOLD BY

EFFINGHAM WILSON & CO.,

Publishers, Printers, Booksellers, Binders, Engravers, and Stationers,

11, ROYAL EXCHANGE, LONDON.

TO WHICH IS ADDED A LIST OF

TELEGRAPH CODES,

VALUABLE BOOKS of REFERENCE essential to COMMERCIAL ESTABLISH-
MENTS and PUBLIC COMPANIES,

GUIDE BOOKS for TRAVELLERS, &c., &c.

In addition to the Works enumerated in this Catalogue, THE BOOKS OF ALL OTHER
PUBLISHERS may be had at this Establishment immediately on their Publication.

EFFINGHAM WILSON & CO. undertake the printing and
publishing of Pamphlets and Books of every description upon
Commission. Estimates given, and Conditions of Publication
may be had on application.

June, 1891.

WILSON'S LEGAL AND USEFUL HANDY BOOKS.

Law of Bills, Cheques, Notes, and I O U's.
Fifty-fifth Thousand. The new Law. By JAMES WALTER SMITH, Esq.,
LL.D., of the Inner Temple, Barrister-at-Law.   Price 1s. 6d.

Joint-Stock Companies (including the three Acts of 1890).
New and Revised Edition. Twenty-first Thousand. By JAMES WALTER
SMITH, Esq., LL.D.   Price 1s. 6d.

The Law of Private Trading Partnership (including the 1890 Act).
Twenty-fifth Thousand. New and Revised Edition. By JAMES WALTER
SMITH, Esq., LL.D.   Price 1s.

Master and Servant. Employer and Employed.
Fifteenth Thousand. By JAMES WALTER SMITH, Esq., LL.D.   Price 1s. 6d.

Husband and Wife.
Engagements to Marry, Divorce and Separation, Children, &c.   By JAMES
WALTER SMITH, Esq., LL.D.   (Entirely New Edition.)   Price 2s. 6d.

Law of Trustees.
Their Duties and Liabilities. New and Revised Edition. By R. DENNY
URLIN, Esq., of the Middle Temple, Barrister-at-Law.   Price 1s.

The Investment of Trust Funds.
By R. DENNY URLIN, Esq.   Price 1s.

Law of Wills.
A Practical Handbook for Testators and Executors. By C. E. STEWART,
Esq., M.A., Barrister-at-Law.   New and Revised Edition.   Price 1s. 6d.

How to Appeal against your Rates
(In the Metropolis). · By A. D. LAWRIE, Esq., M.A., Barrister-at-Law.
Price 1s.

How to Appeal against your Rates
(Outside the Metropolis). By A. D. LAWRIE, Esq., M.A., Barrister-at-Law.
Price 1s.

The Stockbroker's Handbook.
A Practical Manual for the Broker, his Clerk, and his Client.   Price 1s.

The Juryman's Handbook.
By SPENCER L. HOLLAND, Barrister-at-Law.   Price 1s.

Income Tax; and how to get it Refunded.
By ALFRED CHAPMAN, Esq.   Price 1s.

Inhabited House Duty: How and when to Appeal.
By ALFRED CHAPMAN, Esq.   Price 1s.

Law of Water and Gas.
By C. E. STEWART, Esq., M.A., Barrister-at-Law.   Price 1s. 6d.

WILSON'S LEGAL AND USEFUL HANDY BOOKS.

The Juryman's Handbook.
By SPENCER L. HOLLAND, Barrister-at-Law. Price 1s.

Hoare's Mensuration for the Million;
Or, the Decimal System and its Application to the Daily Employment of the Artizan and Mechanic. By CHARLES HOARE. Price 1s.

Ferguson's Buyers' and Sellers' Guide; or Profit on Return.
Showing at one view the Net Cost and Return Prices, with a Table of Discount. Price 1s. Bound in Leather. Price 2s.

House-owners, Householders, and Lodgers their Rights and
Liabilities as such. By J. A. DE MORGAN, Esq., Barrister-at-Law. Price 1s. 6d.

Bills of Sale.
By THOS. W. HAYCRAFT, Esq., Barrister-at-Law. Price 2s. 6d.

The Law relating to the Sale and Purchase of Goods.
By C. E. STEWART, Esq., Barrister-at-Law. Price 1s. 6d.

Schonberg's Chain Rule:
A Manual of Brief Commercial Arithmetic. Price 1s.

The Local Government Act, 1888.
New Edition. By R. DENNY URLIN, Esq., Barrister-at-Law. Price 1s. 6d.

Houses and Lands as Investments.
With Chapters on Mortgages, Leases, and Building Societies. By R. DENNY URLIN, Esq., Barrister-at-Law. Price 1s.

From School to Office.
Written for Boys. By F. B. CROUCH. Price 1s.

Pearce's Merchants' Clerk.
An Exposition of the Laws regulating the Operations of the Counting House. Sixteenth Edition. Price 2s.

Commercial Handbook and Office Assistant.
By MICHAEL CROWLEY, Chartered Accountant. Price 1s.

Double Entry; or, the Principles of Perfect Book-keeping.
By ERNEST HOLAH. Price 2s.

The Solicitors' Clerk. The ordinary Practical Work of a Solicitor's
Office. By CHARLES JONES. Price 2s. 6d.

Powers, Duties, and Liabilities of Directors under the Companies
Acts 1862—1890. By T. W. HAYCRAFT, Esq., Barrister-at-Law. Price 1s. 6d.

Pocket Dictionary of Mining Terms.
Second Edition. By PHILIP MILFORD. Price 1s.

AGER'S TELEGRAM CODES.

THE DUPLEX COMBINATION STANDARD CODE.
Consisting of 150,000 Words.

With a DOUBLE Set of Figures for every Word, thus affording opportunity for each Figure System of Telegraphing to be used. Every word has been carefully compiled so as to avoid both literal and telegraphic similarities. *Price* £6 6s.

The extension of these Words to about 45,000 more.

These are published with the view to being either used in connection with the "Duplex," or for special arrangement with the Figure System for PRIVATE CODES by agreement. *Price* £1 11s. 6d.

THE COMPLETE DUPLEX CODE,

Of 195,000 Words in Alphabetical and Double Numerical Order, *i. e.* the above two Codes bound together. *Price* £7 17s. 6d.

Ager's Standard Telegram Code of 100,000 Words.
Compiled from the Languages sanctioned at the Berlin Telegraph Convention, 1885. Price £5 5s.

Ager's 10,250 Extra Code Words.
Following in Alphabetical and Numerical Sequence those in the Standard Code. Price 15s.

Ager's Standard Supplementary Code for General Merchants.
The 10,250 Words with sentences. In connection with Dr. Ager's Standard Code. Price 21s.

Ager's Telegram Code.
Consisting of nearly 56,000 good Telegraphic Words, 45,000 of which do not exceed eight letters. Compiled from the languages sanctioned by the Telegraph Convention. Third Edition. Price £2 15s.

Ager's Alphabetical Telegram Code.
The Code Words in sequence to the 150,000 Code Words in the Duplex Standard Code. In accordance with the Telegraph Convention Rules. Price 25s. Two or more copies 21s. each.

Ager's Telegraphic Primer. With Appendix.
Consisting of about 19,000 good English and 12,000 good Dutch Telegraphic Words from Webster's and Picard's Dictionaries. Some 12,000 of these have sentences, so that it is the cheapest Code ever published. Price 12s. 6d.

Ager's South African Mining Share Telegram Code.
Affording special facilities for Telegraphing Mining Transactions of South Africa, with instructions for Buying, Selling, and Quotations of Shares. Price 4s. 0d.

THE GENERAL AND SOCIAL CODE,
In which the Code Words and Sentences are alphabetical. *Price* 10s. 6d.

Wilson's Blank Telegram Code.
Consisting of 6000 good English Telegraphic Words, and arranged in a convenient form for making up a Private Code. Price 7s. 6d. net.

TELEGRAPH CODES.

Clauson-Thue's A. B. C. Universal Commercial Electric Telegraphic Code,

Adapted for the Use of Financiers, Merchants, Shipowners, Brokers, Agents, &c. Fourth Edition. Price 15s. net.

Clauson-Thue's A. 1 Universal Electric Telegraph Code,

For the Use of Financiers, Merchants, Shipowners, Underwriters, Engineers, Brokers, Agents, &c. Price 25s. net.

Hawke's Inland and Foreign Telegram Code.

Price 1s.

Lawrie's Universal Pocket Code,

For Private and Business Telegrams. By R. NORTHALL-LAWRIE, M.A. Price 7s. 6d.

General and Mining Code.

For the use of Mining Companies, Mining Engineers, Stockbrokers, Financial Agents, and Trust and Finance Companies. By C. ALGERNON MOREING and THOMAS NEAL. Price 21s.

Rohde's Code Words and Terminal Key:

10,000 tested words for Telegraph Codes arranged for use in Tables, so that three or more sentences, quotations, &c., may be telegraphed together in one word. Second edition. Price 31s. 6d.

Scott's Shipowners' Telegraphic Code.

Sixth Edition (1885). Price 17s. 6d. net.

Stockbrokers' Telegraph Code.

Price 5s. net.

Sutherland's K. K.

The Complete Code for Agents, Bankers, Brokers, and Shippers. Published 42s.; 25s. net.

Telegraph Code,

For combining in one word the date of a Telegram sent, that of the last one Despatched, and that of the latest one Received. Price 21s.

The "Ironscrap" Telegraph Code.

Adapted for the Special Use of the Old Iron and Metal Trades. Compiled by GEORGE COHEN, SONS, & Co. Price 42s.

Universal Mining Code,

For the Use of Mining Companies, Mining and Civil Engineers, Merchants, Agents, Shippers, Manufacturers, and all engaged in Mining affairs. By JAMES STEVENS, M.E., Member of the North of England Institute of Mining and Mercantile Engineers, and R. SYDNEY CORBETT. Price 42s.

Watkins' Ship-broker's Telegraph Code.

Price £4 4s. net.

Whitelaw's Telegraph Cyphers. 310,200 in all.

Two or more copies.

202,600 words, French, Spanish, Portuguese, Italian, and Latin. Price	.	.	.	.	150s. each net.
(This price will shortly be increased to £10.)					
25,000 English words	.	.	.	.	40s. ,, ,,
42,600 German ,,	.	.	.	.	50s. ,, ,,
40,000 Dutch words .	.	.	.	.	50s. ,, ,,

310,200

MEYER'S TELEGRAPH CODES.

Meyer's Standard Grain Code
Consists of 20,000 well-selected and arranged phrases in use in the Grain Trade. Price 35s.

A New Code in English, Spanish, and French.
These Codes are designed to enable English Merchants and Manufacturers to meet the growing competition in Foreign Markets, by providing them with a means of international correspondence. In each of these Codes the same cipher word is attached to the identical phrase carefully translated.

THE ENGLISH EDITION.

The British and Foreign Trade and Shipping Code. Now ready.
This Code contains business phrases of every description, and a SPECIAL and COMPLETE CHAPTER ON CHARTERING. Price 30s. per copy.

The same description answers for the FRENCH EDITION, entitled—

Le Code Télégraphique Universel. Now ready.
It is identical in phrases and ciphers with the English and Spanish Editions. Price 30s. (or 37·50 francs).

THE SPANISH EDITION is entitled—

El Código Telegráfico Anglo-Español, and is now ready.
It is identical in phrases and ciphers with the English and French Editions, and may be used in conjunction with them. Price 30s.

The International Mercantile Telegraph Code
Contains 14,000 well-selected business phrases, suitable for Merchants and Brokers, Exporters and Importers of Produce and Manufactures. Price 25s.

The Commercial Telegraph Code.
This book contains 14,000 sentences, suitable for Merchants and Brokers, Exporters and Importers of Produce, and Manufacturers. Price 25s.

The Appendix Telegraph Code
Contains 4380 blank German Ciphers not exceeding 10 letters, and arranged in tables, *each word having a consecutive number attached.* By means of a few manuscript additions and headings, the purchaser can make a special Code for his own private requirements with very little trouble. This book will be found very useful to Manufacturers. Price 25s.

The Commercial and Appendix Combined Code
Is formed by the "Commercial Code" and "Appendix Code" being bound up in one volume. Price £2 10s.

The General Telegraph Code
Contains 15,000 ciphers not exceeding 10 letters, with well-compiled sentences attached. This book contains a very full list of articles of commerce and their various qualities, also of Government and Railway Stocks and Shares. Price 10s. 6d.

Anglo-American Cotton Code.
Thirty-sixth Edition. The pages relative to quality, staple, market, crop, and receipts, of this revised edition, have been considerably enlarged. CONTINENTAL BUSINESS has been also fully provided for. Price £2 2s.

NEW PUBLICATIONS.

Threadneedle Street, a reply to " Lombard Street,"

And an alternative proposal to the One pound note scheme sketched by Mr. Goschen at Leeds. By ARTHUR STANLEY COBB. Price 5s.

Hutchison's Practice of Banking.

Fourth and Concluding Volume. Demy 8vo., about 550 pages, cloth. Price 15s.

SUMMARY OF CONTENTS.—*Precedents* :—Banking Company's Memorandum and Articles of Association—Building Society Forms—Deposit of Deeds—Mortgaging of Property and Ships—Conveyancing—Bill of Sale—Leases—Bonds and Debentures—Assignments—Guarantees—Power of Attorney—Miscellaneous Forms—Agreements, Authorities, and Undertakings—Indemnities—Declarations—Promissory Notes, Bills of Lading, Warrants, Brokers' Undertakings, Loan and Hire Agreements—Bankruptcy Forms—Wills—Auditors' Certificates, &c., &c.— With Addenda to Vols. II and III, bringing down the Law and Practice of Banking to present date.

The Rules and Usages of the Stock Exchange,

Containing the Text of the Rules and an explanation of the general course of business, with Practical Notes and Comments, and a full exposition of all decided Law Cases affecting the Stock Exchange. By G. HERBERT STUTFIELD, B.A.Oxon., Barrister. Price 5s.

The Money Market Primer and Key to the Exchanges.

With Fifteen Full-page Diagrams. By GEORGE CLARE. Price 5s.

The Solicitor's Clerk.

A Handy-book upon the ordinary Practical Work of a Solicitor's Office, with precise instructions as to the procedure in Conveyancing matters and the Practice of the Courts. By CHARLES JONES. Price 2s. 6d.

Bookkeeping.

By GÉRARD VAN DE LINDE, F.C.A., F.S.S. (Fellow and Joint Auditor of the Institute of Chartered Accountants in England and Wales). PART I.—In connection with the three primary Books of Accounts, viz. Journal, Cash Book, and Ledger, leading up to Trial Balances. PART II. —In connection with Closing Entries, Balance-Sheet, and Profit and Loss Accounts, Companies' Accounts, Fundamental distinction between Capital and Revenue. PART III.—In connection with General Banking. PART IV.—In connection with Colonial and Foreign Banking ; also the Accounts of the Bank of England. Price 3s. 6d.

Jackson's Book-keeping.

A Check-Journal; combining the advantages of the Day-Book, Journal, and Cash-Book; forming a complete System of Book-keeping by Double Entry; with copious illustrations of Interest Accounts, and Joint Adventures; and a method of Book-keeping, or Double Entry by Single. By GEORGE JACKSON, Accountant.

Twentieth Edition, with the most effectual means of preventing Fraud, Error, and Embezzlement, in Cash Transactions, and in the Receipt and Delivery of Goods, &c.   Price 5s., cloth.

Robinson's Share and Stock Tables;

Comprising a set of Tables for Calculating the Cost of any number of Shares, at any price from 1-16th of a pound sterling, or 1s. 3d. per share, to £310 per share in value; and from 1 to 500 shares, or from £100 to £50,000 stock.

"These excellent and elaborate tables will be found exceedingly useful to bankers, public companies, stockbrokers, and all those who have any dealings in shares, bonds, or stocks of any and every description."—*Daily News*.

Seventh Edition, price 5s., cloth.

The Ancient Gold Fields of Africa from the Gold Coast to Mashonaland.

Compiled from the Archives of Ancient and Modern Nations, with Plates and Plans of the utmost interest.   By J. M. STUART.   Price 10s. 6d.

Burgon's Life and Times of Sir T. Gresham,

Including notices of many of his contemporaries. By JOHN WM. BURGON, Esq. Offered at the *reduced price of* 10s.   In two handsome large octavo volumes, embellished with a fine Portrait, and 29 other Engravings.   *Published at 30s.*

Doubleday's Financial and Monetary History.

A Financial, Monetary, and Statistical HISTORY OF ENGLAND, from the Revolution of 1688 to the present time; derived principally from Official Documents. By THOMAS DOUBLEDAY, Author of 'The True Law of Population,' &c., &c. In 1 vol., 8vo.   With Supplement, bringing the work down eleven years later.   Price £3 3s., cloth.   Very scarce.

Redress by Arbitration ;

Being a Digest of the Law relating to Arbitration and Award.   By H. F. LYNCH, Esq., Solicitor.   Price 5s.

Howarth's Our Clearing System and Clearing Houses.
By W. HOWARTH, F.R.Hist.S., &c. Price 2s. 6d.

Hutchison's Practice of Banking ;

Embracing the Cases at Law and in Equity bearing upon all Branches of the Subject.   By JOHN HUTCHISON.   Volumes II and III.   Price 21s. each.   Vol. IV.   Price 15s.

Journal of the Institute of Bankers.
Monthly. 1s. 6d.

§

Barker's Trade and Finance Manual,

A Book of Reference on matters relating to Trade and Finance, with coloured Maps. 2 Vols. Price 6s. each.

Haupt's Arbitrages et Parites.

Traité des Opérations de Banque contenant les usages commerciaux, la théorie des changes et monnaies et la statisque monetaire de tous les pays du globe. Par OTTOMAR HAUPT. Septième édition. Price 10s. 6d.

The Investor's Ledger,

With a few Hints on Keeping it. Contents:—1. Share Calculation Table. 2. Register of Investments. 3. Monthly Diary. 4. Bought and Sold. 5. Interest and Dividend Account. 6. Profit and Loss. 7. Trust Investment Act, 1889. 8. Stamp Act, 1888. Third Edition. 1s. 6d.

Investment Table :

Showing the Actual Interest or Profit per cent. per annum derived from any purchase or investment at rates of Interest from 2½ to 10 per cent. 2s.

Cariss's Book-keeping by Double Entry :

Explaining the Science and Teaching the Art. By ASTRUP CARISS. Second Edition. Price 6s.

Lewis's Tables for finding the Number of Days,

From one day to any other day in the same or the following year. By WILLIAM LEWIS. Price 12s. 6d.

Cummins' 2¾ per Cent. Interest Tables

On £1 to £20,000 for 1 to 365 days. Price 5s.

Ellis's Rationale of Market Fluctuations.

" A compendium of shrewd observations on the nature and causes of fluctuations in market prices, whether they arise from market influences or more general causes. By ARTHUR ELLIS. Third Edition. Price 7s. 6d.

Royle's Laws relating to English and

Foreign Funds, Shares and Securities. The Stock Exchange, its Usages, and the Rights of Vendors and Purchasers. With 400 References to Acts of Parliament and decided cases, and an Analytical Index. By WILLIAM ROYLE, Solicitor. Price 6s.

English Weights with their equivalents in Kilogrammes,

Calculated from 1 lb. to 1 ton by pounds, and from 1 ton to 100 tons by tons. By F. S. STEWART. Price 3s. 6d.

Dillon's History and Development of Banking in Ireland,

From the Earliest Times to the Present Day. Price 6s.

Bankruptcy Accounts.

How to prepare a Statement of Affairs in Bankruptcy. A Guide to Solicitors and others. Price 2s. 6d.

Stock Exchange Book-keeping.

By ROBERT WARNER, Stock Exchange Accountant. Price 2s. 6d.

Kinmond's Universal Calculator.

For obtaining in a few figures the Cost of any number of Articles at any Price, and the Interest of any Sum for any Time and any Rate. Price 2s. 6d.

Pulbrook's Companies' Act, 1862-86;

Stannaries' Act, 1869; Life Assurance Companies' Act, 1870, and other Acts relating to Joint-Stock Companies. With Analytical References, a very copious Index, and the Rules in Chancery. Tenth Edition. By ANTHONY PULBROOK, Solicitor. Price 6s., cloth.

Questions on Banking Practice.

Revised by, and issued under the sanction of, the Council of the Institute of Bankers. Third Edition. Price 3s. 6d.

Dollar and Sterling Exchange Tables.

Compiled to facilitate Exchange Calculations at the finer rates at which Eastern business is now done. 2s. 6d. to 3s., 3s. to 3s. 6d., and 3s. 6d. to 4s., advancing by Sixteenths of a Penny. Price 6s. each.

Rutter's Exchange Tables between England, India, and China.

With new Intermediate Rates of thirty seconds of a Penny per Rupee, six-teenths of a Penny per Dollar, and one quarter of a Rupee per Hundred Dollars; also New and Enlarged Tables of Premium and Discount on Dollars, of Bullion, and of indirect Exchanges between England, India, and China. By HENRY RUTTER. Price £1 10s., cloth.

Rutter's General Interest Tables

For Dollars, Francs, Milreis, &c., adapted to both the English and Indian Currency, at Rates varying from 1 to 12 per cent., on the Decimal System. By HENRY RUTTER. Price 10s. 6d.

Duncan's Manual of British and Foreign Tramway Companies.

Containing Abstracts of Accounts and Traffic Tables of the principal Companies. By W. W. DUNCAN. Published annually. Price 5s.

Duncan's Manual of British and Foreign Brewery Companies.

Containing Abstract of Accounts, Brewery Statistics, and Brewer's Directory. Published Annually. Price 2s. 6d.

Nash's Sinking Fund and Redemption Tables.

Showing Investors the return offered by Securities in the shape of Interest, Drawings, Redemptions, Terminable Annuities. Second Edition. By R. L. NASH.   Price 7s.6d.

The United Kingdom Stock and Share-brokers' Directory for 1890,

Containing list of Members and Firms of the London Stock Exchange, and London Brokers not being Members thereof; also Brokers of the Provincial Cities and Towns.   Price 4s. 6d.

Burdett's Official Intelligence ;

Being a carefully compiled *précis* of information regarding British, American, and Foreign Stocks, Corporation, Colonial, and Government Securities, Railways, Banks, Canals, Docks, Gas, Insurance, Land, Mines, Shipping, Telegraphs, Tramways, Water-works, and other Compauies.   By HENRY C. BURDETT, Secretary of the Share and Loan Department, Stock Exchange.   Published Annually under the sanction of the Committee.   Price 42s.

Poor's Manual of the Railroads of the United States,

Showing their Mileage, Stocks, Bonds, Cost, Traffic, Earnings, Expenses, and Organizations, with a Sketch of their Rise, Progress, Influence, &c.   Together with 50 Maps and an Appendix, containing a full Analysis of the Debts of the United States and of the several States, published Annually.   Price 31s. 6d.

Hankey's Principles of Banking.

Its UTILITY and ECONOMY; with Remarks on the Working and Management of the Bank of England. By THOMSON HANKEY, Esq., a Director and formerly Governor of the Bank of England.   Fourth Edition.   Revised as regards the Working and Management of the Bank by CLIFFORD WIGRAM, Esq., a Director of the Bank.   Price 2s. 6d.

Wilson's Author's Guide.

A Guide to Authors; showing how to correct the press, according to the mode adopted and understood by Printers.   On Sheet.   Price 6d.

Ellison's Cotton Trade of Great Britain.

Including a History of the Liverpool Cotton Market and the Liverpool Cotton Brokers' Association.   By ARTHUR ELLISON.   Price 15s.

Ham's Customs Year Book.

The new List of Imports and Exports, with Appendix, and a brief account of the Ports and Harbours of the United Kingdom.   Published annually.   3s.

Ham's Inland Revenue Year-Book.

The recognised book of Legal Reference for the Revenue Departments.   Published annually.   Price 3s.

Ham's Warehousing Regulations,
With Notes, 1891. Price 3s.

Bosanquet's Universal Simple Interest Tables,

Showing the Interest of any sum for any number of days at 100 different rates, from ⅛ to 12½ per cent. inclusive; also the Interest of any sum for one day at each of the above rates, by single pounds up to one hundred, by hundreds up to forty thousand, and thence by longer intervals up to fifty million pounds—with an additional Table showing the Interest of any number of pounds for one quarter, half-year, or year, at each of the above rates, less income tax from one penny to one shilling in the pound. By BERNARD TINDAL BOSANQUET. 8vo, pp. 480. Price 21s., cloth.

Shaw's Fire Surveys;

A Summary of the Principles to be observed in estimating the Risks of Building. By Captain SHAW, C.B., of the London Fire Brigade. Third Edition. Price 2s. 6d.

Garratt's Exchange Tables,

To Convert the Moneys of Brazil, the River Plate Ports, Chili, Peru, California, and Lisbon (Milreis and Reis, Dollars and Reals, Dollars and Cents), into British Currency, and vice versâ, at all rates of Exchange that can be required, varying by eighths of a penny. New and Revised Edition. By JOHN and CHARLES GARRATT. Price 10s. 6d., cloth.

Bank and Stock Exchange Anecdotes.
Edited by "A LAME DUCK." Price 1s.

Crosbie and Law's Tables for the Immediate Conversion of Products into Interest, at Twenty-nine Rates, viz.:

From One to Eight per cent. inclusive, proceeding by Quarter Rates, each Rate occupying a single Opening, Hundreds of Products being Represented by Units. By ANDREW CROSBIE & WILLIAM C. LAW, of Lloyds, Barnetts, and Bosanquets Bank, Limited. Second Edition, improved and enlarged. Price 12s. 6d.

Cohn's Tables of Exchange
between England, France, Belgium, Switzerland, and Italy. By M. COHN. Price 10s. 6d.

Schultz's Universal Dollar Tables,
Epitome of Rates from $4.80 to $4.90 per £, and from 3s. 10d. to 4s. 6d. per $, with an Introductory Chapter on the Coinages and Exchanges of the world. Price 10s. 6d.

Schultz's Universal Dollar Tables.
Complete United States Edition. Covering all Exchanges between the United States and Great Britain, France, Belgium, Switzerland, Italy, Spain, and Germany. Price 21s.

Pamphlets, &c., on Bimetallism.

ALLARD'S ÉTUDE SUR LA CRISE AGRICOLE, COMMERCIALE & OUVRIÉRE ET SES CAUSES MONÉTAIRES EN ANGLE-TERRE. Price 6s.

BULL'S CURRENCY PROBLEM AND ITS SOLUTION. Cloth, 2s. 6d.

BURCKHARDT'S THE CURRENCY PROBLEM. A Proposal for the Rehabilitation of Silver. By Dr. WM. BURCKHARDT. Price 6d.

BARCLAY'S SILVER QUESTION AND THE GOLD QUESTION. Third Edition. Price 5s.

CAZALET'S BIMETALLISM AND ITS CONNECTION WITH COMMERCE. By EDWARD CAZALET. Second Edition. Price 6d.

CRUMP'S REVIEW OF THE POSITION AND PROPHECIES OF THE BIMETALLISTS. By ARTHUR CRUMP. Price 2s. 6d.

FORSSELL'S APPRECIATION OF GOLD, AND THE FALL IN PRICES OF COMMODITIES. By HANS FORSSELL. Price 6d.

GIBBS AND GRENFELL'S BIMETALLIC CONTROVERSY. A Collection of Pamphlets, Papers, Speeches and Letters. By HENRY H. GIBBS and HENRY R. GRENFELL, formerly Governors of the Bank of England. Price 5s.

GOSCHEN'S PROBABLE RESULT OF AN INCREASE IN THE PURCHASING POWER OF GOLD. By the Right Hon. G. J. GOSCHEN, M.P. Price 6d.

HAUPT'S BIMETALLIC ENGLAND. By OTTOMAR HAUPT. Price 6d.

SCHMIDT'S SILVER QUESTION IN ITS SOCIAL ASPECT. An Enquiry into the Existing Depression of Trade and the present position of the Bimetallic Controversy. By HERMANN SCHMIDT. Price 3s.

SEYD'S BIMETALLISM IN 1886; AND THE FURTHER FALL IN SILVER. By ERNEST J. F SEYD. Price 1s.

SMITH'S BIMETALLIC QUESTION. By SAMUEL SMITH, Esq., M.P. Price 2s. 6d.

SMITH'S (THE LATE COLONEL J. T.) PROPOSAL FOR THE RESTORATION OF THE INDIAN EXCHANGES, with an Epitome of his reasoning in support of his plan. By an EX-MADRAS CIVILIAN. Price 1s.

VAN DEN BERG'S ENQUIRY INTO THE INFLUENCE OF FALLING EXCHANGES ON THE PROSPERITY OF A NATION. 1s.

IN THE PRESS.

Banker and Customer.
By JAS. WALTER SMITH, Esq., LL.D., Barrister-at-Law.

Law of Bankruptcy.
By C. E. STEWART, Esq., Barrister-at-Law.

County Court Guide.
By CHARLES JONES.

Auditing of Joint-Stock Companies' Accounts,
Showing the Requirements and Responsibilities of Secretaries and Auditors. By JOHN WESTBY GIBSON, LL.D., F.S.S.

Licensing Laws.
By T. W. HAYCRAFT, Esq., Barrister-at-Law.

MISCELLANEOUS LIST.

VALUABLE WORKS OF REFERENCE,
COMMERCIAL, LEGAL, GEOGRAPHICAL, AND STATISTICAL.

Arnould's Marine Insurance.
A Treatise on the Law of Marine Insurance and Average; with References to the American Cases and the later Continental Authorities. By Sir JOSEPH ARNOULD (Puisne Judge, Bombay).
Sixth Edition, in 2 vols., royal 8vo. Price £3, cloth.

Anderson's Practical Mercantile Correspondence.
A Collection of Modern Letters of Business, containing a Dictionary of Commercial Technicalities. Thirtieth Edition, revised and enlarged. By WILLIAM ANDERSON. Price 3s. 6d.

Art of Investing. By a New York Stockbroker. Price 3s.

Bartlett-Amati's Weights, Measures, Moneys, and Interest Tables.
Sixth Edition. Price 3s. 6d.

Bithell's Counting House Dictionary,
Containing an Explanation of the Technical Terms used by Merchants and Bankers in the Money Market and on the Stock Exchange. By RICHARD BITHELL. Second Edition, revised. Price 5s.

Byles' Law of Bills of Exchange, Promissory Notes, Bank Notes, and Cheques.
By the Right Hon. Sir JOHN BERNARD BYLES. Fourteenth Edition. Price 26s.

Bagehots' Lombard Street.
A description of the Money Market. Sixth Edition. Price 7s. 6d.

Banking Almanack (The), Directory, Year-Book, and Diary.
A Parliamentary and complete Banking Directory. Published Annually. Price 10s.

Banker's Clerk (The).
Comprising the Principles and Practices of Banking. Sixth Edition, revised. Price 2s.

Bradshaw's Railway Shareholders' Manual. Published Annually. Price 12s., cloth.

Brown's Money, Weights, and Measures of the Chief Commercial Nations in the World, with the British Equivalents.

By W. A. BROWNE, M.A., LL.D. Sixth Edition. Price 2s. 6d.

Blewert's Tables

For Calculating the Value of the Public Stocks and Annuities, and Investments in all Companies and Adventures where the Capital is converted into Stock. Seventh Edition. Price 7s. 6d.

Buckley's Law and Practice under the Companies Acts, 1862-1890.

Containing Statutes and Rules, Orders, and Forms to regulate Proceedings in the Chancery Division of the High Court of Justice. Sixth edition. Price 34s.

Bunyon's Law of Fire Insurance.

Third Edition. Price 18s.

Castelli's Theory of "Options" in Stocks and Shares. Price 2s.

Crump's Theory of Stock Exchange Speculation. Fourth Edition. Price 10s. 6d.

Crump's English Manual of Banking.

Second Edition, revised and enlarged. Price 15s.

Carter's Practical Book-keeping.

Adapted to Commercial and Judicial Accounting. With Outlines of Book-keeping for Beginners. Sixth Edition. Revised and corrected. Price 8s. 6d.

Chalmers' Digest of the Law of Bills of Exchange, Promissory Notes, and Cheques.

By His Honour Judge CHALMERS. Third Edition. Price 16s.

Cotton's Loans Manual.

A compilation of Tables and Rules for the use of Local Authorities. By CHAS. P. COTTON. Price 5s.

Dunsford's Handbook of Railway and other Securities for 15 Years,

Gives at a glance the Lowest and Highest Prices and Dividends Paid. Published Annually. Price 1s.

Every Man's Own Lawyer.

A Handybook of the Principles of Law and Equity, comprising the Right and Wrongs of Individuals. By a BARRISTER. Twenty-eighth Edition. Price 6*s.* 8*d.*

Foster's Double Entry Elucidated.

Twelfth Edition. Price 3*s.* 6*d.*

Fisher's Railway Accounts and Finance.

An exposition of the Principles and Practice of Railway Accounting in all its Branches. Price 10*s.* 6*d.*

Gibson's Stock Exchanges of London, Paris, and New York.

A comparison. Price 4*s.*

Gilbart's History, Principles and Practice of Banking.

Thoroughly revised and adapted to the Practice of the present day. By A. S. MICHIE, Deputy Manager of the Royal Bank of Scotland, London. Two Vols. Price 10*s.*

Grant's Treatise on the Law relating to Bankers and Banking Companies.

Fourth Edition, with an Appendix containing the Statutes in Force. By CLAUDE C. M. PLUMPTRE, Esq., Barrister-at-Law. Price 29*s.*

Goodfellow's Merchants' and Shipmasters' Ready Calculator.

Exhibiting at one View *the solid contents* of all kinds of Packages and Casks. By J. GOODFELLOW. Price 7*s.* 6*d.*

Giffen's Stock Exchange Securities:

An Essay on the General Causes of Fluctuations in their Price. By ROBERT GIFFEN. Price 8*s.* 6*d.*

Giffen's Essays in Finance.

Second Series. By ROBERT GIFFEN. Price 14*s.*

Giffen's (The) Growth of Capital.

Price 7*s.* 6*d.*

Hamilton and Ball's Book-keeping.

New and Enlarged Edition. Price 2*s.*

Hardwick's Trader's Check Book

For Buying and Selling by the Hundredweight, Ton, or by Measure, &c. Price 2*s.* 6*d.*

Hopkins' (Manley) A Manual of Marine Assurance. One vol., 8vo. Price 18s.

Hopkins' (Manley) Average and Arbitration. Fourth Edition. Price 21s.

Houghton's Mercantile Tables

For Ascertaining the Value of Goods, Bought or Sold by the Hundred-weight, at any price from one farthing to twenty pounds per Hundred-weight; or by the Ton, one shilling to four hundred pounds per Ton. £1 1s.

Inwood's Tables

For the Purchasing of Estates, Freehold, Copyhold, or Leasehold Annuities, Advowsons, &c., and for the Renewing of Leases held under Cathedral Churches, Colleges, or other Corporate Bodies, for Terms of Years; also for Valuing Reversionary Estates, &c.
Twenty-third Edition. 12mo, boards. Price 8s.

Jevons's Money and the Mechanism of Exchange. Price 5s.

Jevons's Investigations in Currency and Finance.

By W. STANLEY JEVONS. Illustrated by 20 Diagrams. Edited, with an Introduction, by H. S. FOXWELL, M.A. Price 21s.

Jordan's Practical Instructions on the Formation, Management, and Winding up of Joint-stock Companies. Price 3s. 6d.

King's Interest Tables,

Calculated at 5 per cent., exhibiting at one glance the interest of any sum, from one pound to three hundred and sixty-five pounds; and (advancing by hundreds) to one thousand pounds; and (by thousands) to ten thousand pounds; from one day to three hundred and sixty-five days. Also, Monthly Interest Tables, Yearly Interest Tables, and Commission Tables. Price 7s. 6d.

Kindell's African Market Manual.

Full particulars of the principal Companies. Price 4s.

Lowndes's Law of General Average (English and Foreign).

By RICHARD LOWNDES. Fourth edition. Price 30s.

Lowndes's Practical Treatise on the Law of Marine Insurance.

By RICHARD LOWNDES. Second Edition. Price 12s. 6d.

Lawson's History of Banking.

Second Edition. One Volume, 8vo. (Scarce.)

Laxton's Builders' Price Book,

Containing upwards of 72,000 Prices, carefully corrected and revised according to the present prices of materials and labour. Published Annually. Price 4s.

Laurie's High-Rate Tables of Simple Interest,

At 5, 6, 7, 8, 9 and ½ per cent. per annum, from 1 day to 100 days, 1 month to 12 months. Also copious Tables of Commission or Brokerage, from one eighth to ten per cent. By JAMES LAURIE. Price 7s.

Laurie's Tables of Simple Interest,

At 5, 4½, 4, 3½, 3 and 2½ per cent. per annum. Also Tables of Compound Interest and Interest on large sums for a single day at the same rate. Price 21s., or, strongly bound half Russia, price 26s. 6d.

Lee's Laws of British Shipping and Marine Assurance.

Edited and thoroughly revised to the present time by JOHN C. BINGHAM, Barrister-at-Law. Tenth Edition. One Volume. Price 18s.

London Banks and Kindred Companies and Firms.

Their Directors, Managers, Capital and Reserve Funds and Dividends. By THOMAS SKINNER. Published twice a year—May and November. Price 2s. 6d.

Louis's Anglo-French Calculator.

A Ready Reckoner for facilitating Trade with France. Price 1s.

Lecoffre's Tables of Exchange

Between France, Belgium, Switzerland and Great Britain; being French Money reduced into English from 25 francs to 26 francs per pound sterling, in Rates each advancing by a quarter of a centime, showing the value from one franc to one million of francs in English Money. 21s.

Macleod's Theory and Practice of Banking.

By HENRY DUNNING MACLEOD. Fourth Edition. 2 Vols. Price 26s.

Macleod's Elements of Banking.

Fourth Edition.   Price 5s.

M'Culloch's Dictionary, Practical, Theoretical, and Historical, of Commerce and Commercial Navigation.

Illustrated with Maps and Plans. By J. R. M'CULLOCH, Esq. New Edition, corrected, enlarged, and improved: including a New Supplement. 8vo, cloth, price £3 3s.; or £3 10s., half-bound in russia, with flexible back.

Merces' Indian Exchange Tables.

A New Edition, showing the Conversion of English Money into Indian Currency, and *vice versâ*, calculated for every Thirty-secondth of a Penny, from 1s. 4d. to 1s. 8d. per Rupee.   Price 15s.

Merces' Indian Ready Reckoner.

Containing Tables of Rates by Number, Quantity, Weight, &c., including fractions of a Maund, at any rate from ½ Pie to 250 Rs.; also Tables of Income, Exchange (1s. 3d. to 1s. 8d.),, Interest, and Commission.   Sixth Edition.   Price 36s.

McArthur's Contract of Marine Insurance.

By CHARLES McARTHUR.   Price 14s.

Martin's Statesman's Year Book ;

A Statistical and Historical Annual of the States of the Civilised World for Politicians and Merchants.   Revised after Official Returns. Price 10s. 6d.   Published Annually.

Merchant Shippers (Export) of London, Birmingham, Wolverhampton, and Walsall,

With their respective Trading Ports and the Class of Goods they customarily ship.   Alphabetically arranged.   Price 15s.

Mathieson's Monthly Traffic Tables ;

Showing Traffic to date, and giving, as comparison, the adjusted Traffics of the corresponding date in the previous year.   Price 6d., by post 7d. Monthly.

Mathieson's Highest and Lowest Prices,

And Dividends Paid during the past six years.   Annually.   Price 2s. 6d.

Melsheimer and Gardner's Law and Customs of the London Stock Exchange,

With an Appendix, containing the Rules and Regulations authorised by the Committee for the Conduct of Business. By RUDOLPH E. MELSHEIMER, Barrister-at-Law, and SAMUEL GARDNER, of the London Stock Exchange. Third Edition. Price 7s. 6d.

Mulhall's History of Prices since the Year 1850.

With Eight Coloured Diagrams. By MICHAEL G. MULHALL. Price 6s.

Mulhall's Dictionary of Statistics. Price 6s.

Moxon's English Practical Banking.

By THOS. B. MOXON, Fellow of the Institute of Bankers. Price 3s.

Newson's Law of Salvage, Towage, and Pilotage.

By HARRY NEWSON, Esq., Barrister-at-Law. Price 15s.

Owen's Marine Insurance.

Notes and Clauses. Third Edition. Price 15s.

O'Gorman's Intuitive Calculations;

Or, Easy and Concise Methods of Performing the various Arithmetical Operations required in Commercial and Business Transactions. Twenty-sixth edition, revised. By C. NORRIS. Price 3s. 6d.

Palmer's Company Precedents, for use in relation to Companies subject to the Companies Acts, 1862 to 1890.

With Appendix containing the Acts and Rules. Fifth Edition. Price 36s.

Palmer's Shareholders' and Directors' Legal Companion:

A Manual of Every-Day Law and Practice. Eleventh Edition. 2s. 6d.

Palgrave's Chairman's Handbook.

Suggestions and Rules for the Conduct of Chairmen of Public and other Meetings. By REGINALD F. D. PALGRAVE, the Clerk-Assistant of the House of Commons. Price 2s.

Prospector's (The) Handbook.

A Guide for the Prospector and Traveller in search of Metal-bearing or other valuable Minerals. By J. W. ANDERSON. Price 3s. 6d.

Parity of Indian Government Paper with Rupees.

From Rs. 80 to Rs. 109⅞. Price 8*s*.

Porter's Laws of Insurance : Fire, Life, Accident, and Guarantee.

By JAMES BIGGS PORTER. Price 21*s*.

Pixley's Auditors ;

Their Duties and Responsibilities under the Joint-stock Companies and other Acts. Fifth Edition, Revised. Price 10*s*. 6*d*.

Rae's Country Banker: his Clients, Cares, and Work.

From an Experience of Forty Years. Price 7*s*. 6*d*.

Rance's Tables of Compound Interest,

For every ¼ from ¼ to 10 per cent., and for every year from 1 to 100 years. Second Edition. By THOMAS GEORGE RANCE. Price 21*s*.

Ready Reckoner (National) :

A Series of Commercial Tables for all Trade Purposes, with Profit and Discount Tables and Wages Calculator. Price 3*s*. 6*d*.

Rentzsch's Indian Exchange Tables.

Enlarged Edition. From 1*s*. to 1*s*. 5*d*. Price 15*s*.

Stock Exchange Weekly Official Intelligence.

Compiled under the superintendence of the Secretary of the Share and Loan Department, and under the authority of the Committee. Subscription £2 per annum. By post, £2 5*s*. Single copies 1*s*.

Simmonds's Dictionary of Trade Products,

Commercial and Manufacturing; with the Moneys, Weights, and Measures of all Nations. Price 3*s*. 6*d*.

Sound Investments for Small Savings.

By G. BARTRICK-BAKER. Price 1*s*. 6*d*.

Skinner's Directory of Directors.

A List of the Directors of the Joint-Stock Companies of the United Kingdom, and the Companies in which they are concerned. Published Annually in January.. Price 10*s*.

Skinner's Stock Exchange Year-Book.

Containing a Digest of Information relating to the Joint Stock Companies and Public Securities known to the Markets of the United Kingdom. Published Annually—December. Price 15*s*.

Skinner's Mining Manual.

Published Annually. Price 10s. 6d.

Thomas's Interest Tables,

From 1 to 100 days, and from 1 to 3 per cent. per annum by eighths per cent. Calculated by Decimals. By WILLIAM HENRY THOMAS. Price 21s.

Thom's Interest Tables,

At 6, 5, 4½, 4, 3½, 3, 2¾, and 2½ per cent. Edited by CHARLES CUMMINS. Price 21s.

Urquhart's Dues and Charges on Shipping in Foreign Ports :

A Manual of Reference for the use of Shipowners, Shipbrokers, and Shipmasters. Sixth Edition. Price 25s.

Vogel's Practical Mercantile Correspondence. French-English.

A Collection of French Letters and Forms with Explanatory Notes. Price 4s. 6d.

Williams and Lafont's French and English Commercial Correspondence.

A Collection of Modern Mercantile Letters in French and English, with their Translations on opposite pages. Second Edition. Price 4s. 6d.

Warren's Blackstone.

Blackstone's Commentaries, systematically Abridged and adapted to the existing state of the Law and Constitution, with great Additions. By SAMUEL WARREN, Esq., Q.C. 1856.

Second Edition, in post 8vo, cloth. Price 18s.

Watts's Law of Promoters of Public Companies.

By NEWMAN WATTS, of Lincoln's Inn, Barrister-at-Law. Price 5s.

Whist :

"CAVENDISH'S" LAWS AND PRINCIPLES STATED AND EX-PLAINED AND ITS PRACTICE ILLUSTRATED. Fifteenth Edition. Price 5s.

"CAVENDISH'S" WHIST DEVELOPMENTS: AMERICAN LEADS AND THE PLAIN-SUIT ECHO. Price 5s.

CLAY'S LAWS OF SHORT WHIST, AND A TREATISE ON THE GAME. Price 3s. 6d.

POLE'S PHILOSOPHY OF WHIST. An Essay on the Scientific and Intellectual Aspects of the Modern Game. Price 3s. 6d.

Willich's Popular Tables for ascertaining,

according to the Carlisle Table of Mortality, the Value of Lifehold, Leasehold, and Church Property, and various useful and interesting Tables. Price 10s. 6d.

BADEKER'S CONTINENTAL GUIDE BOOKS.

Great Britain. With 14 Maps and 24 Plans. Price 10s.

Belgium and Holland. With 12 Maps and 20 Plans. Price 6s.

The Rhine from Rotterdam to Constance. With 29 Maps and 21 Plans . Price 6s.

Northern Germany. With 25 Maps and 33 Plans. Price 7s

South Germany and Austria. With 13 Maps and 28 Plans. Price 7s.

The Eastern Alps, Including the Bavarian Highlands, the Tyrol, &c. With 21 Maps, 10 Plans, and 7 Panoramas. Price 8s.

Greece. With 6 Maps and 14 Plans. Price 10s.

Switzerland. With 35 Maps, 9 Plans, and 9 Panoramas. Price 8s.

Paris and its Environs. With 10 Maps and 30 Plans. Price 6s.

Northern France. With 9 Maps and 25 Plans. Price 7s.

Southern France, From the Loire to the Spanish and Italian Frontiers, including Corsica. Price 9s.

Northern Italy and Corsica. With 8 Maps and 32 Plans. Price 6s.

Central Italy and Rome. With 7 Maps and 29 Plans. Price 6s.

Southern Italy, Sicily, Malta, Lipari Islands, Carthage, and Athens. With 25 Maps and 16 Plans. Price 6s.

Palestine and Syria. With 18 Maps and 44 Plans. Price 20s.

London and its Environs, Including Brighton, the Isle of Wight, &c. With 4 Maps and 15 Plans. Price 6s.

Norway and Sweden. With 21 Maps and 9 Plans. Price 9s.

Lower Egypt, with the Fayum and the Peninsula of Sinai. With 16 Maps, 30 Plans, 7 Views, and 76 Vignettes. Price 16s.

Traveller's Manual of Conversation, English, French, German, and Italian. Price 3s.

www.ingramcontent.com/pod-product-compliance
Lightning Source LLC
Chambersburg PA
CBHW030820270326
41928CB00007B/827